Daughter of the Palms

Growing Up in the South Sudan

by Kathleen Adair

DORRANCE
PUBLISHING CO
EST. 1920
PITTSBURGH, PENNSYLVANIA 15238

Dorrance Publishing Co
585 Alpha Drive
Suite 103
Pittsburgh, PA 15238
Visit our website at *www.dorrancebookstore.com*

ISBN: 978-1-4809-3515-0
eISBN: 978-1-4809-3538-9

Chapter One

Hills are mountains to a child, teeth are tusks. Memories are such fickle things, and yet I cherish them, remembering not so much each tiny detail as the whole experience, the feeling, taste, aroma of those early childhood years in Africa.

Dolieb Hill cannot compare to the hills of Missouri, or even a small foothill of the Rockies, but I loved the way it seemed to sweep swiftly up from the banks of the Sobat River and then crest, spreading out into flat savannah land, headed for the horizon hanging in the distance. I felt it was my personal mountain.

I also claimed as mine a hippo tusk. The ivory curve fit perfectly over my shoulder, and I cradled it there, imagining a tiny infant cuddling by my chin. I dressed it in doll clothes and tenderly nursed it through many of my childhood years. When in adulthood I, in a nostalgic moment, asked my mother if she remembered my huge tusky doll, she said, "Oh, you mean that old hippo tooth?" and described it with her hands about ten inches apart, while I, in disbelief, stretched out my arms to indicate its length. That childish perception lingers yet.

Dolieb Hill is a mission station that was started by Presbyterian missionaries in 1902. By the time my mother and father arrived with little Eddie in 1946, joining my grandparents already stationed in the South Sudan, the operation was fairly well-established. Dad was fresh out of seminary, and Mom had completed half of a nursing program, which she left to accompany Dad overseas. For my father, who had spent his own childhood years in the Sudan, returning was a long-awaited homecoming, but my mother was in a state of culture shock, from which she did not fully recover for at least half of the seventeen years they spent there.

Dolieb Hill. Although we lived on several different mission stations, this is the one which occupies that special home-place in my heart. Established in the Upper Nile Province of the South Sudan, it is built in the middle of flat savannah and scrubby thorn forests. Mud huts dot the banks of the river, and tall palms pose in small groups near the water. It is the land of the Shilluk people, and I was Nya Tha Took, Daughter of the Palms.

The story of my birth there, in a mud hut, is often recounted at family gatherings. Although I am the second child of Bill and Martha Adair, I was the first to be born in Africa. I was expected in the middle of August…but let me share the story in my mother's words, as she wrote the story for me and gave it to me for a wedding gift…

"When our first born was 8 months old, I realized that he would not long be alone. We had been in the Sudan for only one month at the time, and I really thought it was a little unfair of God to allow such a turn of events. The strangeness of the new homeland was still strong with me, language a problem, and we didn't even have our own house yet! We lived with two single missionary ladies.

"As the discomforts of my condition increased, the boarding bit became more and more of a trial. One of our benefactors was a very frugal person, and one of her money saving techniques was to serve bread and soup for supper every night. Fresh bread was not baked until the last batch had been consumed, no matter what condition it had reached. The refrigerator was small, no room for bread. So, if it got moldy, the mold was cut off and we ate the remains. In that hot and humid country, the loaves began to spoil from the center, producing a particularly nauseating odor and a gluey consistency.

"Our hostess was also very conservative where bathing was concerned. Although her work with the village schools required that she walk many miles each day in the hot sun, she still limited herself to a sink bath, and her clothing never received even that much attention. The combination of two or three day old clothes and the far gone bread caused me to lose many suppers.

"Fortunately for us, about two months before the baby was expected, a house of sorts was completed for us. There was a cement block unit, which included the kitchen, store room and bathroom. This was attached to a mud walled unit with a thatched roof and a cement floor, which contained a bedroom, a living room, and a dining room. Although the thatched roof kept us cool, the supports were made of unseasoned bamboo and branches, which were instantly infected with wood borers, which immediately became busy reaming out tunnels, creating a fine dust which fell constantly. Little stinging ants also frequented the rafters, feeding on the borers and falling with the dust onto all that dwelt below. Another overhead nuisance was the bevy of bats that dangled from the ridgepole by day, and spent the night swooping back and forth, feeding on the mosquito hordes.

"It was our good fortune to have a missionary doctor stationed at Dolieb Hill. When he did my eight month exam, and discovered that the baby was headed in the wrong direction, he advised me to go to Khartoum, in the north Sudan, to the government for delivery. I was understandably dismayed. Bill could not be released to go with me, and I would have to make a 500 mile trip alone, leaving my first child, now thirteen months old, behind. I did, however, see the wisdom of the suggestion, and we decided that I would take the next plane from the provincial capital of Malakal, scheduled to leave in three days.

"I had always heard that when you are upset it is good to do some hard work to take your mind off your worries, so I got out the grass knife and began to scythe the grass around the house. Too ungainly to squat as the native people did, I spent a number of hours doubled over, hacking at the grass.

"The next day was Sunday. Sitting on the ground among the Shilluk women at church I began to feel more than just uncomfortable, I was downright sick! By lunchtime it was apparent that I was in the early stages of labor, and would not be waiting for Tuesday's plane.

"Dr. Rhoode was able to turn the baby manually, but he could give no reassurance that it would stay in that position. He was concerned about how the delivery would go, how much equipment might be needed for the delivery of a premie, and whether he could handle a difficult birth in such a primitive setting. He set two pressure stoves on the dining room table, filled a large pan used for washing clothes with water, and began to heat it. Into this makeshift sterilizer, he put all the obstetrical equipment he had.

"In the middle of these hurried preparations, Bill tried to keep busy and out of the way, pacing back and forth carrying the first aid book, and wishing he could do something useful. Passing the sterilizing apparatus, he noticed a string floating among the equipment. Thinking it had fallen from one of the thatch bundles in the roof, he fished it out and threw it on the floor, where it went unnoticed until the delivery time was imminent and the doctor was nervously checking to see that everything was ready. 'Where's the cord tie?' he suddenly shouted. 'It was here a minute ago!' Bill sheepishly retrieved the 'thatch string' from the floor, and put it back in the pan to boil.

"With the instruments ready, Dr. Rhoode began to consider whether anesthetic could be used. Since the pressure lantern was the only available light, and highly flammable ether the only available pain reliever, we did without.

"Kathleen Susan Adair made her appearance at 3:30 a.m. on Monday, July 14, 1947. She weighed in at 5 lbs. 2 oz. Her skinny wrinkled body and spidery arms and legs shivered, and her tiny head was crowned with a mass of dark hair. She was not very beautiful, but we loved her anyway. We were all a little concerned about her prematurity, and how she would fare in such primitive surroundings. Later that day we found her lying in a pool of blood! The infamous cord tie had slipped!

"Frantically, Dr. Rhoode put together an improvised incubator with a pressure lamp for heat and a blanket tented over the bed to keep the heat in. Into this we put her tiny weak body, and prayed that it would work. If Kathy could have talked, she probably would have said what she says now when things get tough. 'Oh, I'll survive.' Needless to say, she did.

"One day, while I was lying in bed, feeding baby Kathy, a bat landed on the bed near her head! I jumped up, cutting off her food supply, and leaving her to the mercies of the bat! When I realized what I had done, I was horrified that my reflexes could so easily overpower my protective instincts, but once again, she survived.

"At five months of age, Kathy weighed only ten pounds. Although she was small, she was strong and wiry, and could spend long periods of time balanced on her forehead and toes, playing with her toys. Then she learned to crawl. From that time on, I often found her parked beside the mud wall, picking off pieces of mud and eating them. When I questioned Dr. Rhoode about this, he just sighed, and said that something must be missing from her diet. He seemed unconcerned, but I had seen how those walls were made: ten parts ordinary earth, three parts clay soil, two parts sand, two parts straw, four parts water, and two parts cow manure. The senior missionary on the station often stood watching her and shaking his head. 'She'll never live to be a year old,' he said.

"But she did make it to her first birthday, and shortly after that we went to London, where Bill was to study at the University of London for a year. The contrast between Kathy and the overstuffed and rosy-cheeked English babies was immediately apparent. Everywhere we went, Kathy was petted and cooed over: such a tiny, pale, fragile looking, beautiful baby! The Londoners sympathized with her difficult first year, deep in the disease ridden continent of Africa, and tried valiantly to make up for it. They fed her sweets and choice tidbits of rationed items, for which she returned smiles and chortles and dutifully learned the mechanics of polite English childhood.

"Besides the appeal of her tiny size and fragile appearance, Kathy charmed everyone at 1 1/2 years by singing, in recognizable fashion, the words and tunes of several choruses. Thriving on all the attention and extra goodies, she never ate mud in England. Perhaps it just didn't taste right!" So my mother recorded the first years of my life.

Many years after leaving the Sudan, I still feel strongly the attachment to my birthplace. Something in my center, in my soul, still resonates with memories; the elegant waltz of the palm leaves with wind, whispering and rustling a soothing melody, which so often lulled me to sleep. And oh, the stark and, lonely beauty of the flame trees! In a land where even Nature's beauty is harsh, the acacias are a startling sight. Spreading wide their thinly leafed, thorn-studded branches, they offer intricate and deeply colored blossoms, that demand acknowledgement of fragile beauty, set against a rather barren backdrop of gray green grassland.

Attracted by the delicate shape of the acacia flowers, I often climbed the trees to try to snatch one from their thorny limbs. Though this was rarely a success, I felt the need to claim their beauty as my own, only much later coming to appreciate their function within that ecosystem.

The slow, meandering presence of the river touched me too, and now links that distant time to the present. The sight of the mighty Mississippi in these later years still transports me to the banks of the Sobat, where I played hide and seek among the bamboo groves, and upon which I learned to drive an outboard motor when children my age, in America, were begging to be allowed to just steer the family car.

Standing by the river, I smell again the damp, musky fragrance of water hyacinth, feel the gentle sally of the wind upon my cheek, and the keen sting of spray across my face. Across the river in my mind, idly cruises the beguilingly ugly, yet elegant pelican. It's intoxicating!

Chapter Two: Debur

Debur was a splendid looking man by anyone's standards, but to me he was like Superman. His skin was a deep glossy black, as most Nilotic tribesmen are. He was tall and sinewy, built for walking across the vast savannah, his shoulders wide and well-defined from rowing his dugout canoe, for which prowess he had earned a small reputation. Across his shoulder blades and back were sculptured the tails of scorpions, carved there when he was initiated into manhood in the Shilluk tribe. Similar scars stood in line across his forehead.

I once saw a young girl having these tribal marks made on her body. It was gruesome. She sat mute and motionless, but for an occasional wince, while each tiny piece of skin was pierced with a fish hook, pulled away from the body, and sliced with a razor blade. This grizzly process was repeated until a bloody design was formed, which was then rubbed with manure and mud. Each cut, after it had gone through several stages of infection and finally healed, would leave the desired scar, and the design would be permanent.

I understood the ornamental nature of the scorpion tails, and the tribal marks on the forehead, but the fish outlined with the same marks on Debur's arm perplexed me. I tried in very broken Shilluk to ask him about it, and finally appealed to my father to act as translator. It seemed that the fish was there to remind him of a particular fish that was taboo for him to eat. Having told us this, he began to grin and gesture to his other arm. Asked to elucidate, he said with sparkling eyes and cunning looks, that he was going to have a chocolate cake done on the other arm. Remembering his dramatic reaction when I had coaxed him into trying some, we all began to chuckle. He despised it, running to the door to spit it in the dirt, and holding his hand over his mouth as if he had been poisoned!

I often tried to get Debur to taste our unfamiliar food, and in turn ate the native food when I followed my young Shilluk friends to their village homes. One day we all ganged up on him and got him to put some ice cream in his mouth. He had no concept of cold, much less freezing, and nearly went into shock! He thought his mouth was burning, though he knew there was no fire. Holding his head, and gasping like a fish on land, he ran to the sink to spit it out, and realized that it was gone! Once assured that he was not, indeed, burned, he ran out to the garden and brought in the reluctant gardener, O Libe. "You must try this wonderful new food," he said, smiling craftily as he held the spoon to O Libe's lips. O Libe nervously opened his mouth to protest, and Debur shoved the ice cream in! He was not disappointed. O Libe moaned and groaned and danced around the room, holding his mouth and clutching his head, while Debur doubled over with hilarious laughter, tears pouring down his face as he enjoyed the joke that we had so recently played on him.

Debur worked for us as a houseboy for many years beyond those that I can recall. I used to follow him around as he worked, squatting beside him as he scrubbed our clothes in a tisht, which resembled an enormous pie pan, or watching in fascination as he put glowing coals into the old black iron to heat it, and then filled his mouth with water, and blew it out over the clean clothes to dampen them for ironing.

The people of Debur's village must have begged him for stories of how the strange white people lived. My mother recalls the first time they saw her in high heels. Unable to contain their amazement and mirth, they tittered and giggled and finally gave in to outright laughter as they pointed to her feet and nudged their companions to have a look. Sometimes, they reacted with fear rather than laughter or amazement. The Shilluk's primitive belief in spirits colored much of their living, imbuing everything with the fear that angry gods and spirits would be displeased and mete out retribution. I once made a tape recording of Debur singing as he worked, thinking that he would be amazed to hear himself. But when I played it for him his jaw dropped, his eyes began to roll and he took off as if pursued by demons. Perhaps he thought he was, for surely his soul had been trapped in the machine!

Although we had very little common language, there never seemed to be a barrier between Debur and me. I loved him, and felt that he cared about me. And yet, how little I knew him. Like the Superman that he was to me, he had an entirely separate identity as part of a culture that I could never fully participate in. I have a picture of myself at age 6, standing outside our home in Dolieb Hill, holding his hand. He is wearing a white western style shirt and shorts, his houseboy uniform. In another shot, he stands by his own native hut, leopard skin around his waist and a spear in his hand. What a schizophrenic existence it must have been for him; beloved servant in our world and respected rower and drummer in his own.

Chapter Three: Shulla Land

❧

As a child, Debur represented the Shilluk people to me, and the love I felt for him extended to them. In addition, respect for them has grown in later years, as I have sought to understand more about those among whom I grew up. They are a beautiful people, tall and smoothly black, with great physical endurance and features that often combine well-defined cheekbones and high foreheads with wide flared nostrils and heavy lips.

The tribe traces its origins to the Lake Victoria region of Africa, now known as Uganda. According to their spoken traditions, it was here that Nyibong, the god-hero and first king of the Shilluk people, lived with his mother, who was part crocodile, and his brother. The two brothers often quarreled violently. Following one such incident, Nyibong was driven from home. Alone, he journeyed north, along the upper Nile, in search of a new home. As he went, he gathered into his following all the indigent populace. Where these were lacking, he used his great magic to turn animals into human subjects. Finally, satisfied that his kingdom was impressively large, he settled at the mouth of the Sobat River, a tributary of the Nile.

Today, the Shilluk tribe numbers some 80,000, stretched loosely along 150 miles of the Nile and some 50 miles up the Sobat. In spite of the fact that they are so widely dispersed, these people do have sense of unity as a tribe. They are an organized nation, the only one of the Nilotic tribes of the South Sudan that has a king.

Individual villages are built around extended family units with a patriarchal lineage. There may be several wives, as well as older female relatives whose husbands are no longer living. The center of each village is the cattle barn, around which all activity and daily living revolve. For all of the river tribes, cattle are bride wealth. Hump shouldered, poorly formed beasts though they are, they are the standard of wealth, position and prestige.

Every Shulla male takes the name of his favorite bull when his initiation rites have confirmed before all of the tribe that he is truly a man. They assumed, as a matter of course, that this was a universal custom, and when my father arrived in the Sudan, already married, they asked him what bull's name he had taken. At loss for an answer, he finally replied that his father had once given him a white bull which had had its horns cut off. He was immediately christened, Oshoda Nybong, the white bull with no horns.

Around the cattle barn, which is a round Tukul, just like the houses, only larger, the family units are clustered. Each has a cooking hut, and a sleeping hut, connected by a small courtyard enclosed with a fence of grass mats, or kaal, which offers some minimal protection from wild animals at night. A mat, or sometimes a skin, also hangs across the two foot by three foot door of each tukle.

Building a house is a communal project, in which both men and women participate, mixing the clay with straw and manure and plastering the mixture onto a bamboo frame. Singing and chanting as they work, they secure rafters to the frame wall with rope made from the sisal cactus, and stomp the mud floor to a smooth, hard surface which can be swept clean with a twig broom. A specialist is called in to complete the roof. Thatching is a job which not everyone is skilled at, so there is a great deal of prestige afforded to those who master it.

The interior decoration of the house usually consists of sleeping mats and skins hung on the walls, along with the skins worn for dances. These are usually civet cat or sheep. Since the Shilluk are not hunters, the presence of a leopard skin is unusual, and highly prestigious. Longhaired dancing wigs may also decorate the walls.

Often the man of the house will have a special pillow, which he uses to keep his exotic hairdo from becoming mussed at night. This is actually a small branch, with twigs for legs, resembling a small sawhorse. Lying on his sleeping skins, papa balances his neck on the back of the "pillow," and so keeps his hairdo intact. Since some of these masterpieces take years to create from hair grown long and matted, keeping their shape is an important issue.

Often manure is rubbed into the hair to change the color to red, or more often a dull orange. When my youngest brother was born with a head full of naturally red hair, the Shilluk were amazed, and envious, pestering my mother for the secret formula so that they could copy it.

One of the most intricate hairdos is the bat wing, which to us resembled a pair of Mickey Mouse ears. As the hair is grown, it is continually compressed and heated, until it feels almost like felt. At this stage it can be shaped, until, eventually the bat wings are created.

Near the door of the sleeping area of a hut, in readiness for any emergency, the family spears are kept. There may be several types. A flat, arrow-like head is common for fighting, and for killing snakes or wild animals which may bother the cow herd. For fishing, however, a special spearhead is used, shaped like a pyramid with small curved hooks protruding from it. These prevent the spear from slipping back out of the flesh, once something has been stabbed. Though not hunters, the Shilluk are great fishermen, using both large nets, and these fearsome fishing spears, which besides being effective fishing tools are capable of leaving frightful wounds when used to gouge an enemy! My mother tells of a man who hiked more than ten miles to the Dolieb Hill clinic, holding the shaft of such a weapon, with the wicked hooks buried in his gut!

In the cooking hut, various woven baskets are hung, many full of dried foods. These are often made by the villagers, both men and women. There are baskets for storing grain and dried meat or fish, as well as specially shaped baskets used for tossing the grain to separate it from the chaff. Leaves of various local plants are the most common materials used for weaving, but rope baskets are also made, and these hang from the rafters, providing airy storage for various sizes of gourds, which have been cut in half, and serve as the family dinnerware. The women also make clay pots for cooking and beer making, as well as clay pipe bowls shaped like the heads of animals; some inspired by a private artistic fantasy, others based on a living animal. A huge round metal pan for frying completes the set of cooking utensils.

Cooking is done over an open fire, usually just outside the door of the cooking hut, except in the rainy season, when frequent wet weather forces everyone indoors. In spite of the four inch hole in the roof, through which some few strands of smoke do manage to escape, when cooking is done indoors, every cooking hut is a smoky den, presided over by bleary-eyed women.

Also in the cooking hut, in a place of honor, is the sacred family spear, which is handed down through generations, having once belonged to the original ancestors who settled there by the river in the time of Nyibong. Ancestry and genealogy are immensely important in the Shilluk culture, and are traced through the paternal side of the family. Youngsters can often recite the names of grandfathers many generations back.

Knowing who you are descended from is, to the Shilluk, a part of understanding who you are. Traditional ways of living are highly valued, passing down from one generation to the next with little change. Progress, as defined by the Western world, is very slow in this third world country, and those who propose change are often stymied by the widely held belief that, "What is good enough for my grandfather is good enough for me."

Despite this somewhat blasé response to efforts of the early white missionaries to stimulate "progress," some changes have slowly begun to evolve. In 1902, the first missionaries were greeted by a crowd of native "savages" with very little clothing, though the women did wear goat skins, usually a pair of them, tied around the waist and up over the shoulder. By the time my parents arrived in 1946, muslin cloth was available from the Arab traders, and had taken the place of skins.

Underneath the outer cloth, women wear a small beaded apron called an ocien, and an oban, a sort of half-slip tied around the waist. Women tie their cloths over their left shoulder and men over the right. Only an extremely impolite man would pass by a woman on the left side where her cloth is open. Although nudity is common among the Nuer and the Dinka tribes, for the Shilluk it is acceptable only in the cattle camps among the men and young boys. Occasionally, in the privacy of the kaal, a woman at work may discard her cloth.

Cloth is not cheap in this society where very little cash is tendered, so it is literally worn until it falls apart. Within a few weeks from the initial purchase, everyone's cloth takes on the same grayish brown color, resembling the local clay, and making it impossible to achieve a fashion statement with the color of your costume. There are, however, many styles of beads, and different ways to wear them. Compared to the intricate beaded collars worn by Dinka women, further to the south, the Shilluk style is quite restrained. But, even so, what is in fashion in bead wear this year may indeed be passé the next.

When we received missionary barrels of old clothes, it was an occasion for great excitement, and often astonishment, as my mother handed out whatever had arrived. We were sometimes just as amazed as the Shilluk were, especially when fur coats were sent to the heart of hot and humid Africa! After one such handout, we went to church the next day and had to restrain our laughter in order not to offend the old man who came with an old girdle wrapped tightly around his chest!

For people whose existence is shaded in grays and browns, colored fabric is something of a marvel. On festive occasions, a little piece of colored fabric that could be used as a flag was a great prize. I can remember a large group of swaying, singing women, surging up around our door, on their way to a dance, begging Dandwong (my mother) for a colorful remnant.

The colored chalk, which the teachers used in the mission school, was also a hot item. We have slides of the exotically feathered golden crested crane, stretched in splendor across the blackboard to illustrate a story for beginning readers. In the villages, those who could get a hold of it often used it to draw large and colorful murals on the inner walls of their homes, depicting scenes of local wildlife, which were quite exquisite in their beauty and detail.

These are a primitive people who exist day to day in an arduous environment, constantly battling with natural forces to assert their right to exist. The struggle does not diminish them, but rather seems to affirm their identity as people of the land, their only goal that of survival. This acceptance of the difficulty of life, its pathos and joy, beauty and ashes, new life and death, is perhaps an attitude that those of us caught up in the race for progress would do well to cultivate.

Chapter Four: The Launch

At what was, in my time, Abdagadder's Trading Post, where old man Abdagadder had a tin hut with a few basic supplies to sell or barter, the Sobat River merges with that greatest of Africa's waterways, the Nile. We traveled on both in our 14 foot aluminum boats with outboard motors that strained to move more than 25 miles per hour. The eight mile stretch of the Sobat from Dolieb Hill to Abdagadder's was usually fairly uneventful, but once you were on the Nile, there was occasionally other traffic, such as the large paddle wheel steamers that plied up and down its length.

Before outboard motors were available, early missionaries navigated the rivers in houseboats, and even lived on them for long stretches of time while they were settling a new station. One of these old motor launches was moored at Dolieb Hill for a while, when I was about seven. It made a perfect playhouse, with its enclosed cabin. My siblings and I often sneaked down to where it was moored to play, despite strict injunctions from my mother against such activity. One such excursion proved the wisdom of her warnings.

"Let's go down to the river!" I said one day, when things at the house seemed dull, and Mom was working over at the clinic. So off we went, plunging down the hill, planning our imaginary trip.

"We could go to Pibor and visit the Swarts," said Gwen.

"Or Nasir, to see the Gordons," said Ed, who had a crush on their oldest daughter, dating from earlier childhood when he had asked her to "wife" him.

A small group of school boys from the mission school had already begun to straggle after us, as they usually did whenever we left the house. They loved to try out the English they were learning and with staccato accents pronounced, "What time is it now?" "Will you marry me?" "What is your name?"

I was quickly irritated by this intrusion, and offered my standard brush off, "Shockolongobongoshay!" This was just a string of nonsense, and only made the boys laugh as they renewed their efforts to engage in conversation. Once we were actually on the launch, it was easier to ignore the school boys and develop the theme of our game.

"Let's pretend we are shooting crocodiles," said Gwen, "Or hippos! One of those old rogues that goes crazy and attacks people!" We clambered out of the cabin and onto the deck to get a better "aim," edging carefully along the ledge that led past the cabin to the back deck. Suddenly, right behind me, Gwen toppled over the edge and disappeared under the water! Her head bobbed up once, and I struggled frantically to get to a place where I could lean out and reach her!

"Kathy, help me!" she blubbered as she went under again. Gaining a tenuous foothold on the edge of the deck, I grabbed her arm when she breached the surface again, and hung on for dear life!

"Help!" I screamed. "She's slipping!" "If she goes under one more time she'll drown, three times is it," I thought, dredging up this less than useful piece of information in a moment of crisis, while a part of me watched in horror as her arms slid through my hands.

In the next second, all of my resentment at the crowd of school boys on the bank was blotted out with overwhelming relief as one of the older boys waded out into the river toward us. Just as her arm slid from my grasp, and her nose sank below the water, he grabbed her, and pulled her safely to the bank. Scrambling off the launch to see if she was all right, my next thought was, "Mom will really whale us if she finds out about this!"

In hurried consultation with my brother, we decided that he would go back to the house to see if Mom was home. Gwen and I shakily made our way up the path, praying that the coast would be clear. When we got to the fence that surrounded the house, Ed was wildly beckoning from the back porch. "Hurry up!" he hissed. "She's still at the clinic. Get those wet clothes off, Gwen, but don't hang them on the clothesline, she'll see them!"

Acutely aware that he was right, we hustled into the bedroom which we shared, and I hung the wet clothes in the back of the closet while Gwen changed. "Are you OK?" I asked. The enormity of what had nearly happened suddenly hit me, and I flopped onto the bed feeling as if a wild rhino had suddenly pinned me to the ground. Again I saw Gwen's face as she sank under the water, and knew again the feeling of total helplessness as her arm slid through my hands!

"I'm all right," Gwen said, in a quavering voice. "I'm all right Kath."

Chapter Five: Time to Eat

"Time to eat! Time to eat!" yelled Ouyiche. I was hovering by the kitchen door waiting for the call, drawn by the tantalizing aroma of his fresh baked rolls: so light and fluffy and fragrantly warm! My mouth was watering at the thought.

Working against the strongly held Shilluk traditions which regarded cooking as women's work, Mom struggled for years to teach Ouyiche the rudiments of western cuisine. His bread was his greatest triumph, and one of our greatest pleasures.

For Ouyiche's wife, and other Shilluk women, cooking was rarely a triumphant experience. For them, it was just a part of the struggle for an existence only marginally above subsistence level. The making of kisra, an obscure relative of the tortilla, for example, was a difficult and time-consuming process. Once the durra (a grain resembling millet) had been grown and harvested, it had to be beaten with sticks to remove the grains from the head of the stalk. These were then placed in a hollowed out stump, and crushed with a large 4-5 foot log, which the women operated like a piston, lifting it high and then smashing it down into the stump until all the grains were cracked open and the hulls lay mixed with the heart of the grain.

The next step was to toss the mixture, bit by bit, high in the air from a basket so that the chaff was caught in the air and carried off. Then the women would get out their special grinding stones, worn smooth and gray from much use, and kneeling behind these, they would place some grain on the bottom stone, fit the top one over it, and leaning forward to increase the pressure, push one stone against the other, pulverizing the grain between them. The result was a coarse, stone ground flour. A mixture of the flour with water made a soupy batter which was cooked like a huge pancake on a large metal pan set on stones over an open fire, and then dipped into fish stew and eaten without utensils.

So much work to produce so little food. No wonder Shilluk women look old before they are twenty! And no wonder Ouyiche was astonished when he first saw fifty pounds of fine white flour in a huge muslin sack in our storeroom. In spite of what appeared to him to be abundance, we had to horde our supply to make it last several months, until we could get to the provincial capital, Malakal, to buy more. Sometimes even there, the supply would be short, and Stavaros, the Greek merchant who ran the store where goods coveted by foreigners and upper class Arabs were imported, would be full of apologies when he couldn't fill our order. Kraft cheese in a can, Lyle's golden syrup, and Marmite were such treasures that I still feel a thrill when I find them in a fancy import store in St. Louis.

But sugar and flour were staples which we could not substitute for. We bought both in fifty pound sacks, which presented some storage problems. In the rainy season, the sugar often clumped together, and had to be broken apart before it could be used, but the flour was even more difficult to keep. About three quarters of the way through the sack, little gray specks would begin to appear. Weevils! Ugh! At first they could be ignored, but as they proliferated, and the ratio of weevils to flour increased, the flavor became less and less palatable.

We had reached this point in the sack one day, and Mom decided we better use up what was there before the weevils totally polluted the flour. "This is the last of our flour," she said to me, "and it's Ouyiche's day off. How about making some bread for us?" As she spoke, she was loading the weavily mess into the huge tishst that the clothes were washed in. "We'll put this out on the chicken coop for a while, so the sun can kill some of the weevils, and then you can make the bread." I was just learning to cook, and had begun to develop a good reputation with the family, so I was thrilled to be given the responsibility of salvaging the last of the flour.

An hour later, there was a clap of thunder, and a sudden squall dumped rain down in sheets. "The flour!" Mom and I shrieked together, and dashed out the back door to try to rescue it.

"You better use it right away," Mom sighed, looking at the gluey mess. "We won't be able to get the weevils out now." So I went to the kitchen, and began to carefully measure and mix. I dissolved the yeast, stirred in the flour and oil, and set it under a towel to rise. Half an hour later I stood in horror, staring at long and fatty wormlike globs of dough, which were sliding over the top of the pan onto the table. I almost expected them to squirm in my hands as I gingerly scooped them back into the pan and began to add a little more of the precious flour. It was still too soft. I was about to add a little more, when Mom came in to check on my progress. "It looks too soft," she said. I nodded. "How in heaven's name did you get so much dough? Did you follow the recipe?"

"Yes," I gulped.

"You couldn't have. You must have put in too much water. Just look at this mess!"

"No I didn't," I said stubbornly, "I put in just what the recipe said."

Obviously Mom didn't believe me. Muttering to herself, she began to stir in the last few cups of flour. I hovered beside her, gulping down sobs, and repeating determinedly that I had followed the recipe. Finally, in exasperation, she said, "Just leave me alone and let me see if I can save this mess."

I retreated in tears, determined not to admit fault for something which I knew I had not done. While Mom stomped furiously around in the kitchen, I went to the old pump organ and banged out every hymn I could play, accompanying myself with the litany, "I did follow the recipe. I did!"

I saw Dad enter the kitchen, and heard Mom's voice rise in anger as she told him what had happened. I set my teeth and rehearsed my repudiation of her story. "I did follow the recipe! I did!" Suddenly the turmoil in the kitchen quieted. I stopped my hymn battering. Mom appeared in the doorway, and I stubbornly lowered my eyes. "I did follow the recipe," I muttered. She approached slowly.

"Yes, I believe you did. I owe you an apology." Caught by surprise, I looked up. "You put in all the water the recipe called for, just like you said." I nodded. "But all the rain water was already in the flour, and neither of us thought of that!"

The rain water! Of course, the rain water! The corners of my mouth began to twitch as I pictured the mound of dough spreading like an enormous cancerous growth. I checked Mom's eyes and noted the beginnings of a gleam of humor. My grin expanded, broke open, and both of us began to chuckle and then to howl with laughter.

Relieved that our clash of wills was resolved, we went back to the kitchen, and together mounded the brackish dough into loaves, which we baked as best we could. It was the most horrible thing that I have ever cooked, but I did follow that recipe!

Chapter Six: The Nile Monitor

A few days ago I entered a ladies' restroom, and was assaulted by the nose-shriveling scent of air freshener. Chug chug, slap, chug chug, slap—suddenly I was in the top bunk of the Nile Monitor, listening to the thud of the motor and the slap of the paddle wheels hitting the water. There are certain things that are quarantined to suddenly transport me back to that earlier part of my life on the other side of the world; the smell of mud by the river, burning weeds in a farmer's field, watching a storm sweep in from the horizon, or even the feel of waxed paper, which so closely resembles the feel of the toilet paper we used.

Memories of traveling by paddle wheel steamer are among my favorites. To spend days at a time on the river, and yet be surrounded by opulent grandeur, was a fantasy come to life. My favorite time was breakfast in the dining room. Busy safragees in their blindingly white jellabiyas, with deep red cummerbunds around their waists and velvety maroon tarbooshes on their heads, moved in gracefully choreographed patterns, offering steaming and fragrant dishes to each guest from a silver platter, and lifting selections to the diner's plate with a deft movement of a pair of silver spoons.

Feeling like a princess, waited on hand and foot, I sat a little straighter, and put on my best company manner, waiting with ill-concealed eagerness for the beverage server. His performance was masterful! Holding a silver pot in each hand, one coffee or tea and one hot milk, he would pour from both at the same time, starting close to the lip of the cup, and then arching up to almost a foot and back down, creating and then erasing two perfect arcs that blended in the filling cup without a drop or a splash. I was awed. Try as I might, I never came near to doing it with the panache he displayed.

One of the particularly wonderful spots on the steamer was the area on the top deck, which was screened in so that one could sit in comfort, not bothered by flies or other insects, and watch the river bank slide by. Sometimes we would plead and beg until Mom would order afternoon tea and biscuits there. It was also here that Mom and Dad ensconced themselves in front of a 1000 piece jigsaw puzzle, much to the amazement of the steamer's staff, which had never seen anything like it!

From the low slung deck chairs we could watch the world meander by on either side; here a Nuer village with women slamming their washing against the stones at the water's edge, and young boys herding cows down to drink; there two men wading through the grass and water hyacinth with spears aloft, ready to plunge them into some unwary fish. Sometimes there would be miles and miles of tall papyrus, almost close enough to touch, with thick spongy stems and tops resembling huge green dandelions, lining the bank with plush greenness.

As we got into the forest area, we saw fewer villages and more animals. Monkeys chattered, birds squawked and dipped out over the river to fish, and even larger animals were often in evidence. Once a family of elephants suddenly appeared from among the trees. The mighty matriarch took violent exception to our passage through her territory, and rushed along beside us, flapping her humongous ears and trumpeting loudly.

We also encountered plenty of hippos and crocs. The hippos always seemed to be greeting us as they wriggled their ears and flipped their piglet-like tails just above the water. The crocodiles, in contrast, were generally stretched lazily on the bank, taking in the rays. Sometimes they slid, with crafty grins, into the water at our approach, but often they didn't seem to notice that we were there at all. Part of the charm of the whole experience was that life went on all along the river's banks, diverse and vibrant, according us less than a blink of acknowledgement before taking up again the rhythm of the river. Passing through, I truly felt that all was right with the world, and of course God was in His heaven.

The Nile Monitor was not actually primarily a passenger boat. It was one of a fleet of post boats, so named because they carried the post, or mail, from the capital city, Khartoum, in the north Sudan, to the outlying provincial areas along the river further south. The longest trip we took was all the way to Juba where we stopped for a day or so before going on by plane to Uganda for vacation.

The post boats also carried supplies which were not readily available in the more primitive areas of the Sudan. In fact they often stopped at Dolieb Hill with loads of fresh bananas or other goods such as grain, flour or canned goods from Europe. Whatever the cargo, it was loaded onto flat barges, which were lashed to the sides of the steamer, making up an ungainly entourage, which was often difficult to maneuver in anything other than a straight line.

The captains of these behemoths were usually northern Sudanese, of Arab descent and volatile nature. I used to think that they must all have congenital hearing loss, or else they assumed that everyone else did, for they seemed to conduct all their daily affairs in a decibel range that verged on being painful. I doubt if sweet nothings were ever whispered in the ears of their lovers; more likely they screamed them at each other. So, imagine the confusion, the cursing and shaking of fists, the frenzied rushing about when a barge would come loose from the main boat! Such bewailing of fate, such loud entreaty to the great Allah, and such slow, slow progress toward a solution! In spite of such insanity, which seemed normal to me anyway, I was deeply disappointed when we began to travel by airplane instead of by post boat.

Middle Eastern Airports, I was to discover later, were even wilder than the post boat experiences. A few years ago, I returned to Africa, traveling with my husband, who had never been outside the United States. No sooner had we disembarked at Cairo airport than I was in heaven, back on African soil! He, however, gazed around in total incredulity at the frenzy that infused everything. People broke into fistfights over someone butting ahead in line, baggage was spread everywhere as it tumbled off of the carousels and people dived for their suitcases and boxes, sure that someone else would get there before they could stake their claim, as well they might! "I've seen better organized riots!" he muttered.

Recently, in a sentimental phase, I made myself a small model of a paddle wheel steamer, with the name Nile Monitor on the side. Living near the Mississippi, it is possible to pay for a ride up and down the river on something very similar to what I remember from Africa. Sometimes in the heat of the St. Louis summer, I go down to the Mississippi river front, where McDonalds has turned an old paddle wheeler into a fast food joint. I sit on the deck and munch on a Big Mac, and suddenly the present fades, the Big Mac becomes British biscuits and tea, the cars parked on the levy are Nuer huts, and passing barges are brought to tow by the side of the steamer in preparation for a trip up the Nile.

Chapter Seven: The Demon

Of the four different houses that we lived in during the seventeen year span of my parents' service in the Sudan, the one at Dolieb Hill is my favorite. It was huge! The center was a large square, divided into three bedrooms on one half and a living room (cum school room) and a dining room in the other half. Surrounding the central core was a wide verandah, with screen from the eves to the low brick wall, leaving it open to cooling breezes, and a cement floor. Jutting out from the verandah on one side was the kitchen, storeroom and bathroom. There was even a small attic above the storeroom, which made a great hiding place for games of hide and seek. Doors from the bedrooms (which we never slept in because the enclosed spaces were much too hot) opened onto the verandah along one side of the house; at one end was a sleeping area separated from the rest by a screen door, and protected from possible rain storms by a large canvas curtain, which was rolled up like an awning most of the time, but could be let down in a hurry when a storm struck.

One summer, when I was in junior high, Mom decided that the curtain was looking pretty shabby and that a family project would be a wonderful memory maker. She organized us into work shifts, to share the job of stitching a new curtain of brightly striped, heavy canvas. Our sewing machine was an ancient Singer, which was operated by a hand turned wheel. It predated even treadle machines. With this contraption, it took several of us to manage the heavy fabric. One person would pull it, one would guide it from the front, and another would laboriously turn the wheel, as inch by inch, we stitched the miles of fabric. Complaining loudly, we nevertheless took our appointed turns, and eventually completed the project, of which we were inordinately proud.

For me, the curtain protected from more than just rain. It also prevented wild animals from peering in at me. Although there were occasionally leopards or hyenas in the garden, it was unusual for them to come close to the Dolieb Hill house. At Atar, this was not the case, but that is another story. I am quite sure that my parents tried to reassure me that nothing was out there waiting for me, but imagination often pays no mind to mere fact. Every time I swung my feet over the side of the bed, I cringed, sure that crocodiles were waiting with jaws agape. The worst ordeal of all was the midnight trip to the bathroom!

How I dreaded the feel of that pressing need to pee, which woke me nightly for a number of years. My first ploy was to try to ignore it, and go back to sleep. Then, I would try urgent pleas to God, who could surely help if He really cared! All else failing, I would finally begin to tentatively call out for Morn or Dad to wake up and give me a flashlight. Then, there was no turning back.

As I inched along that oh so long verandah, I tried to keep my eyes glued to the tiny pool of light the flashlight gave, and silently warded off the lurking evils of each dark bedroom doorway that I passed. I was terrified of looking either to the left or the right, for there were surely unknown spirits loose in the bedroom depths, and if by chance I escaped their notice, the eyes of some nighttime predator would be glowing evilly on the other side of the verandah screen.

Each of us siblings seemed to have a certain animal that we especially dreaded. My older brother Ed dreamed of rabid dogs, but my particular demon was hyenas. I still cannot forget the first night I was awakened in panic by the hideous, half-human cackle of a hyena pack. It became my nemesis, often cursing my dreams.

During the day, I could rationally tell myself that hyenas were cowards, and did not generally attack humans. But at night, they became demonic phantoms which prowled through my dreams, and reduced me to a state of rigid terror! Almost every night during my pre-teen years, I would wake from the nightmare in a cold sweat, gasping for breath. I felt as if I were crushed against the bed smothered by the acrid hyena stench. Snatches of the dream would float around me, merging and reemerging, while I struggled desperately for full wakefulness and the strength to banish them.

The principle demon was a grayish, greenish, hunchbacked, slope shouldered hyena with a long snout, and lips curled back in an evil grimace which revealed ragged, rotten teeth. Its eyes glowed like live goals as it prowled around the house, and I could hear the shib, shib, shib, of the thongs it wore on its feet.

That sinister shib, shib, shib was usually the first hint of the arrival of the monster in my dream world. At the sound I would, as my dream self, scramble from the bed on the verandah, and dash for the bedroom, braving the dangers lurking there, rather than expose myself to those demonic eyes! Above the thudding of my heart, the shib shib shib would grow louder and louder. Then the gloating face would appear above the low brick wall, teeth bared and eyes on fire, searching me out!

I was haunted more often when we lived at Atar than at any other station, even though I was in high school at the time. The house there was not far from a thorn forest, which truly did harbor many wild animals. We quite often found their tracks in the dust just outside the screened verandah. I used to wake up nightly at that house, shivering in my own sweat, and debating with myself as to whether the stench in the air and the grunting noises on the other side of the curtain were human or hyena. The man who collected the waste from the bucket that served as a latrine under our wooden toilet, did his rounds at night, grunting under the load he carried, and smelling much like a hyena, so I always tried to convince myself that it was only him.

One night, I woke as usual in a cold sweat, struggling for breath, and shaking uncontrollably. There was surely an animal on the other side of the curtain! I could hear it panting loudly and periodically emitting low growls. I wanted to scream! I wanted to run! I couldn't move!

"Psst!" Oh, thank God, someone else was awake! "Psst! Kafe! There are two hyenas out there and I think they are going to fight!"

I peered warily out from under my covers, and saw that Ed was creeping slowly toward the screen with a flashlight. He had just reached it when the squall broke! Growling and snapping at each other, the opponents grabbed opposite ends of a bloody mass of flesh and began to fight over it, tugging and growling, and furiously trying to wrench it from each other. When the light from Ed's flashlight hit them, they turned tail and bolted for the forest, the prize still strung between them. "Whew!" said Ed. "Did you see that? " I nodded mutely. "No one will believe this! We saw two hyenas fighting! No one will believe this!" He was right. No one really did. When he tried to tell the family about it in the morning, with me chiming in as if I had been right there at the screen, instead of cowering behind him, we were met with total skepticism. They were sure that they could not have slept through such a ruckus. But they did!

Chapter Eight: The Lion's Head

❧

"Association is coming up next month," Dad said at dinner one night.

"Oh boy! Where will it be?"

"Can we go?"

"Will the Roys be there?"

"Wow! I can't wait!"

"Hold your horses, hold your horses!" Dad laughed. "It will be at Akobo, we're all going, and yes, I think the Roys will be there."

"We can all go! Oh good!"

"How will we get there?"

"Well, Mom and I haven't talked about that yet," Dad said, "but I was just thinking about what we should do for talent night. Last year everyone really liked our singing, and I thought that this year we could make up some funny songs about some of the people who will be there."

"We could sing about Uncle Lowrie's bald head," I said. "Remember that time we gave him a big gourd to wear on his head, and taped hair all over it?" There was a burst of appreciative laughter.

"Let's see," said Dad. "Bald head, umm … maybe a mosquito bit it … umm … A skeeter loves a hairless man," he began to hum a familiar tune and Mom piped up, "On him he's quite at home …"

"Good, good," Dad muttered. "I've got it!"

"A skeeter loves a hairless man/On him he's quite at home/No better pasture can be found/Than Uncle Lowrie's dome.

" Now, here's the chorus…

"Oh, I wish that dome were mine, mine mine, I wish that dome were mine. I wish that dome were mine mine mine, I wish that dome were mine!"

"Terrific!" we yelled, giggling delightedly. "Do it again! Do it again!" and he did, throwing back his head and belting it out like Caruso. By the third repeat, we were all chiming in on the chorus, and he was on a roll!

"How about the time Vern and Harvey were hunting and the lion walked right up to the jeep?" suggested Mom.

"Good idea, good," said Dad, beginning to mumble to himself, "Harvey and Vern, Vern and Harvey…"

"Harvey and Vern went hunting," sang Mom…

"OK," said Dad, "let's see…"

"A riding through the night/Along came Leo Lion/And boy did they turn white!/Oh, I wish that hunt were mine, mine, mine." We took it from there, and then did it again for a good measure.

"And Milton," said Dad." That time he turned the boat over … something about a sheet of water … umm … let's see." He hummed to himself, and we waited respectfully for the outburst. "I've got the last two lines. He took a sheet of water, and pulled it over his head."

"I know, I know!" cried Mom … "Milton went riding on the river. Poor bum he had no bed. He took a sheet of water. And pulled it over his head!"

We cheered, and joined in the chorus … "Oh I wish that bed were mine, mine, mine…"

What fun we had when Dad was singing! He had quite a repertoire of hilarious songs, which he was more than willing to mutilate to fit the situation, and though most people thought he was a very quiet, gentle person, which indeed he was, he had a well-hidden exhibitionistic bent, which association talent night invariably brought out! Some of my favorite family memories are of us all gathered around the table, working out our performances for the association meeting.

Association was a yearly event, at which all of the missionaries of the Presbyterian Church who were stationed in the South Sudan got together. Everyone traveled to one station, and the grownups struggled with business matters, while the children ran riot, thrilled to have so many kids to play with. To us, the adults were all "Aunt and Uncle," and the children seemed like cousins. It was a huge extended family reunion!

Since the various stations were not close to each other, some travel was often necessary. Sometimes we went by boat, but if the hosting station was not on a river, we had to drive, as we did the year we went to Akobo. It was a two day trip, following a rough trail across the grassland. We had a Land Rover at the time, a British version of a four wheel drive Jeep. Since there was no such thing as a roadside motel, or even strictly speaking, a road, some planning for food and sleep accommodation was necessary.

I was quite impressed with the ingenious rig that Dad came up with. Across the bench-like seats in the back of the Rover, Dad built a wooden frame with doors like those that go down into a cellar. Under this could be stored all the luggage, plus food for the trip. On top of this he put a mattress, so that the four of us kids could ride there during the day, and at night we could line up side by side like the nine men in a boarding house bed in one of Dad's songs. We were all in a dither, wanting to try it out days before the departure date, running around begging to help, but mostly getting in the way. Finally, we had only twenty-four more hours to endure.

When the sun's early rays slid under the curtain of the sleeping porch, and struck my face, I rubbed my eyes, rolled over, and tried to grab hold of the delicious sense of anticipation that lapped at my consciousness. Mom and Dad were already up. "It's today!" I said. "We're going today!" I popped up and skipped to the bedroom, Gwen not far behind me. Bobbing in excitement, we dressed in record time, and ran out to watch the loading of the Land Rover. Everything was ready. The trapdoors on Dad's contraption were being closed and our riding spot looked inviting. The boys ran to join us, and we clambered up over the tailgate and took up our perches. In a few moments Mom brought the last of the supplies, and we were off!

It was not what you would call a restful trip. We bounced and jolted along the rough path that was barely wide enough for the Rover to follow. As we got further out into the savannah, the villages became less frequent, and the path got rougher and rougher. Dad wrestled with the wheel, trying to steer a course that would at least miss the largest pits, while we bounced around in the back like so many juggler's balls, grateful that the mattress was between us and the hard flat seats. After one terrific jolt, Gwen landed with a yelp, and said impishly, "Whew! I flew so high I thought I was an angel!"

On either side of the path, the grass grew five feet tall, obscuring the view, and leaving to the imagination the multitude of wildlife which we knew inhabited the area. For a while Dad rode on the front fender with his gun, peering over the grass to try and spot a tiang (relative of the antelope), which we sometimes killed for meat. There were fat gray bustards, ostrich and golden crested cranes. Dad reported wildebeest in the distance. When the height of the grass took a dip, we could see a herd of giraffe, leisurely grazing the lower branches of thorn trees. At that point, Dad took the wheel, and veered off the path to get a closer look, which sent them skimming over the grassland, long necks stretched forward, legs moving in perfect symmetry. As I write, I see them clearly flashing across my memory in wild, free and beautifully muscled movement.

A little before dusk we stopped for our picnic supper. By letting down the tailgate of the Rover, Mom could reach under our makeshift bed and recover the food. Munching on our sandwiches, thrilled with the recent excitement of the chase and the reunion still ahead, we could barely contain ourselves. Much too excited to even consider sleeping, on we went.

As darkness thickened, the tall grass took on a rather more threatening quality. "What's that?" Mom said in a strange voice. I strained my eyes down the path and saw two shimmering eyes rather high off the ground. "Good night!" muttered Dad. "It seems awfully tall." It was by now too dark to see anything but those eyes. They didn't move.

"Should I get the gun?" Mom whispered hoarsely.

"No, I'll be able to shine the headlights on it soon, that'll scare it," said Dad uncertainly. He switched to the high beams and crept slowly toward the strange looking eyes. Then, as the lights hit the face, a huge road grader stood illuminated! There was a moment of stunned silence, and then all six of us burst into relieved laughter. In the whole of the South Sudan there were probably not more than ten of those machines, and here was one parked in the middle of what could hardly even be called a beaten path!

We drove on, a little spooked by the encounter with the grader, in spite of the outcome. Dad was beginning to yawn, and talk about stopping for the night, when, at the side of the road ahead, a set of eyes appeared. He stopped, and then in stupefied silence we watched a lioness and her three cubs emerge from the grass, amble across the road, and disappear in the grass on the other side.

"Well," said Mom," we're not sleeping here."

"What if there are more of them?" I screeched. "What if they come after us?!"

"Don't worry," Dad tried to reassure me. "As long as we're in the Rover, all they'll smell is the gasoline. That's how the lion got so close to Vern and Harvey. It never smelled them, it was after the tiang they had tied to the hood. The smell of the gasoline confused it. We'll be fine."

We drove on for a while, and finally did stop to sleep. I was not at all sure that the gasoline story was true, and rumbled around in the makeshift bed, trying to settle down, until my siblings all squawked, and Mom resorted to threats of spanking. I turned on my side, thinking that perhaps I could stuff my head under my pillow. Suddenly, in the window of the door in front, I saw a bunch of dark fur! I screamed, and scrabbled to the back of the bed, oblivious to the outcry my siblings raised. Glancing again at the front seat, sure that the entire head of a lion would now be visible, I saw, there against the window, where he had tried to get comfortable to sleep, my dad's hairy head!

Chapter Nine: Miriam

From the vantage point of adulthood, I am prepared to swear that my mother never changed shape when she was pregnant, although three times after I was born it supposedly occurred, and I have brothers and sisters to prove it.

I am a little clearer on the actual event of Miriam's birth. The entire family, by then four children, ages 3-8, traveled up to Egypt, to the American Mission hospital in Tanta, where there was an American doctor who had gone to school with my dad at the American School for Missionary Children in Alexandria, Egypt. My mother had had enough of primitive childbirth methods. So we combined vacation time with the delivery of the youngest Adair.

My first glimpse of Miriam was when Mom brought her from the hospital to the house we were staying in. I had a cold, and had to wear a cloth mask to protect her from my germs. As soon as I saw her wrinkled newborn face under a halo of red down, I was in love. Although I was dying to hold her, she seemed so fragile that I was afraid of dropping her. During the first few days, I spent many vigilant hours perched by her bed, watching her sleep, and admiring the occasional wave of her tiny, perfectly formed hands and feet. Gradually I grew braver, and began to hold and cuddle her. By the time we returned to the Sudan, I felt like a pro.

What fun I had putting Miriam in my wicker doll carriage and prancing up and down the verandah. She was a wriggly baby, not easy to keep a hold of, but I had lost all fear of dropping her long ago. Secretly, I was delighted that most of my brothers and sisters were too young to hold her for long, and I took full advantage of the few years between us, volunteering for every child care chore, right down to changing diapers. No proud mother could have been more thrilled with her new baby than I was with Miriam!

One night I struggled into wakefulness, full of a sense of foreboding. Intuitively I felt that something was wrong, and seeing the light in Miriam's room, felt a stab of fear. The low muttering of voices told me that Mom and Dad were both up, so it was more than a dirty diaper or an early morning feeding. I longed for the courage to creep out of bed, but the velvet blackness of the night was smothering me, and I could hear the hideous cackling of hyenas in the distance.

Eons later, the thick blackness began to dissipate with the first rays of the sun, loosening also the clammy grip of fear that had immobilized me. I crept out of bed and into Miriam's room, where, in the semi-darkness I could see that Mom and Dad were packing.

"What's wrong?" I whispered, startling them both.

"Miriam is sick, honey, and we're going to take her to the doctor in Malakal."

I heard the suppressed tears in Mom's voice, and felt again the cold finger of fear on the back of my neck. Malakal! We only took people to Malakal who were seriously ill, though the government hospital there was not really much to boast about. "You hold Miriam for a while," Mom continued, "while I finish packing." I held up my arms to tenderly receive the baby, and sat with her in my arms, rocking and crooning, as I often did, "Miriam Louise sings with the breeze …" until her tiny red head relaxed on my arm. "Please God, make my baby well," I prayed, "Please God, please …"

Dad stayed with us at the station, while someone from the other mission family stationed at Obel with us, took Mom and Miriam to Malakal. For several days we waited. A cloud of apprehension hung over me, giving the world around me a sort of faded, surreal quality, while my own inner reality stood stark and terrifying. "Please God, make my baby well …" It was all I could cling to, day and night. Then one morning, I woke to find Dad standing by my bed.

"Miriam has gone to be with God," he said gently.

"You mean she died?!" I whispered hoarsely.

"Yes dear, she died last night. Uncle Alan came back late to let us know."

I tried to absorb it, but could not. "But I asked God to make her better! I prayed and prayed! He should have made her better!"

"I prayed for that too," Dad said, patting me gently, "but God doesn't always change things to make them the way we want them."

"But how could God take my baby?" I sobbed. "I can't stand it!"

Dad brushed tears from his own eyes, and reached out awkwardly to try to offer comfort. "We have to go to Malakal now," he said. "Mommy needs us."

When we reached the guest house in Malakal, my first thought was, "Where is she? I want to see her!" I followed my mother down the hall to the bedroom, and there she was, sleeping quietly in a little white box. Mom was crying softly. So was I. She looked so alive, and I longed to pick her up and cuddle her close. I watched intensely, trying to catch some flutter of an eyelid or twitch of a tiny finger that would make it all a lie. There was nothing.

By the time we headed for the cemetery, I was choking with grief and anger. Enveloped in my own thick shroud of emotion, I was oblivious to all attempts others made to offer comfort. Watching the casket, with my baby in it, being lowered into the ground, I wished that they would just bury me too.

The days following the funeral brought little relief. Everything reminded me that she was gone. No gurgling baby talk woke me in the morning; no tiny person slumbered through the Sunday sermon on my lap. There was no one to sing to, no cherubic face playing peek-a-boo over Mom's shoulder. At the early age of eight, I knew despair. For days I sat rocking in the corner where I had often snuggled Miriam to sleep, whispering over and over to myself, "Miriam Louise sings in the breeze ..."

My mother wrestled with her own loss. Her letters to her own mother at the time are full of her sense of abandonment, and her concern for what was happening to the physical body of her beautiful baby, lying under the ground. "I feel such emptiness of arms and heart," she wrote. "The Shilluk have an expression for this which, literally translated, means, 'to hold your heart.' That's what I feel like I am doing."

Gradually, as she stifled her own feelings, Mom tried to help me deal with mine, insisting that I participate in normal daily activities. Some weeks passed, and one day she came to me and said, "Have you noticed that all the Shilluk mothers have been coming to see me and to cry with me?" I nodded. "They are coming because they can't believe that a child of Oshoda and Dandwong could die. They didn't think that kind of thing happened to white people, but only to them. They have children that die all the time, you know. They thought I was different from them, but now they have seen that my children can die too, and that I hurt just like they do." I nodded again, struggling to understand. "Maybe," I said, "Maybe that's why God made Miriam an angel?"

Chapter Ten: Goodbye

"Dear Mom,

At the present time, I am a prime example of unvictorious living. We got the kids (the two older ones) off to school, and it was mighty hard. Certainly not as hard as losing Miriam, but hard enough. It was harder for Kathy than for Eddie. Eddie cried some, and said, 'I shouldn't be crying, I'm a big boy.' Right then he didn't look like a very big boy to me. Kathy howled ..."

What a treasure my grandmother left us in the bundles of letters postmarked Khartoum, Sudan, with a return address of Dolieb Hill via Malakal. For several years before 1956, my mother's letters to Grandma are full of references to planning for our schooling. Several times the Presbyterian Mission considered the idea of starting its own school for missionary kids from the Sudan. Mom variously reports plans for school in Asmara, Ethiopia, Khartoum, or even at one point, Dolieb Hill. In the meantime, families purchased correspondence courses called Calvert School, and mothers took on the task of beginning their children's education. It was not, from my point of view, the optimum arrangement, and was certainly a struggle for Mom, who had no training in teaching, but she wanted to put off boarding school as long as possible.

From an early age, I knew that boarding school was in the future, though I had no clear idea what that meant. Dad, having some pleasant memories of boarding school himself, tried to reassure us all, but Mom only knew it could not be put off forever, and she dreaded it. I was in the third grade when it was decided that the next year Ed and I would go to the American School for Missionary Children, called Schutz, in Alexandria, Egypt, where many of the older children from mission families in the Sudan were enrolled.

Dad told us stories about his grade school years there, and at the yearly association meetings we quizzed the older kids who were home for the summer. It all sounded thrilling! So many kids to play with, and real teachers! How I longed for the day when I would be one of the "big kids."

Preparations began months before the actual departure. School clothes that Mom had ordered long before from Montgomery Wards arrived, and I was in heaven! I'd never had so many clothes! Each piece had to have a nametag, and I labored mightily over the stitching of them into the necklines and waistbands with careful minute stitches that I had learned from taking needlework classes with the Shilluk girls at the girl's school down at the Palms.

Mom was worrying that we wouldn't be ready in time, that our school work had not been up to par, and a host of other concerns, not the least of which was how we would weather the nine month separation, without her help and guidance.

One day she came by as I was struggling to pull the sheets up on my bed. "You're going to have to learn to make your bed better than that before you go to Schutz," she said. I sighed, and watched her miter the corners with perfect hospital technique. It was a couple of days before we were to leave, and part of me wished that being unable to make a decent bed would indeed be grounds for canceling the future. Fear had begun gnawing at the corners of my mind, edging out the excitement and anticipation with ragged threads of panicky uncertainty.

I was beginning to realize that in order to go to Schutz, I would have to leave home! It seemed unthinkable. I tried to imagine being somewhere other than home, without my family, but there was nothing to hang an image on. I wanted to grab back each moment as it scuttled by, to stop the sun as Joshua did in the Bible, to create a Never Never Land, and like Peter Pan, refuse to ever grow old enough to go to school. But things were still getting packed, and no one came to empty the suitcases, and tell me that I didn't have to go. There was no magic fairy dust, nor even, as far as I could tell, a God to send an angel to my rescue. I felt abandoned.

The night before we were to leave, I tossed and turned, wrestling with my pillow, alternately giving way to tears, and trying to weave what threads of encouragement I could together to keep myself from bursting apart. I bumped into Gwen, slumbering beside me, and to my amazement, she began to slowly rise to a sitting position. Her eyes were wide open, eerily reflecting the moonlight. "Kathy where are you? Kathy where are you?" she rasped. Thoroughly spooked, I sat up too. "I'm, I'm, I'm right here," I stuttered, and shuddered as I realized that in the nights to come she would get no answer to that question. A shadowy outline appeared by the bed, and Mom was leaning over us, and then hugging us both to her, offering what comfort she could for the pain of the coming separation.

My curdled stomach woke me in the morning. I choked on the tears gathering in my throat as I crept from bed and began to grapple with my new traveling clothes. My brain was mush, refusing to focus on the task of adding last minute items to the suitcase. I clung to the thought that Dad was taking us as far as Khartoum, where he would try to get entry visas for us into Egypt. Children who had already been to Schutz had easily received visas for re-entry, but we first timers had not yet been granted the needed papers.

Finally, breakfast attempted and my suitcase closed, there was nothing left to do but say it. "Goodbye," I whispered, nearly strangling Gwen and Tim with frantic hugs. I surrendered to Mom's arms for a minute and then wrenched myself away, resolutely turning my back on my family and my beloved Dolieb Hill. As I shuffled down that hill, I could hear Mom sniffling behind me, but I refused to look back. Stumbling down to the boat, the sound of sobbing was loud in my ears, and I realized suddenly that it was my own. Completely overwhelmed, I gave in to my grief, and began to cry in earnest. Somehow I clambered into the boat, dimly aware that I had done so and that we were pulling away from the bank.

Several miles down the river, huddled into myself, I was startled into reality by Ed yelling, "Hey, that's the Land Rover! It's Mommy! Stop, Daddy, stop!" The boat swung violently toward the bank, where the Land Rover pulled to a stop in a cloud of dust. Mom hopped out, waving frantically. "Good grief!" Dad mumbled. "What on earth is she doing?" We edged up to the bank and Mom came scrambling down, still waving. She had something in her hand. It was Fuzzy Face, my favorite pink teddy bear. "You might need him Kathy," she said, as with a wavering smile she handed him to Ed. I tried to speak, hugged him to me, and broke into fresh sobs. Yes, indeed I might.

Chapter Eleven: Khartoum

⁀⊂⁀

"Look Daddy, we're going to dock right over there!" I said, as the chug, chug, slap, slap of the paddle wheels slowed, and the steamer slid closer and closer to the bank. Cacophonous confusion reigned all over the docks, as we watched. Men were running back and forth, gesticulating wildly, curses flew, and bystanders, waiting for the boat to dock, ducked and dodged, trying to keep out of the crossfire.

I had been to Kosti before, but had never really assimilated it. I tried to now. How different these northern Sudanese were from the Nilotic tribes of the south. Arab ancestry and influence were apparent everywhere. The light brown skin of the workmen swarming over the barges proclaimed it. So did the heavily veiled faces and gracefully draped figures of the women, many heavily laden with bundles of possessions, waiting to board the various steamers. There was a raucous, dusty atmosphere, which seemed to intensify as the sun rose to midday. As we disembarked, loud guttural sounds of Arabic mingled with the braying of donkeys, and even grunting camels. People greeted passengers as they came off the boats with great courtesy, ceremoniously kissed both cheeks, and in the next breath baldly cursed the stumbling of a workman, bent double under a load of freight.

Hesitantly, I scurried down the gangplank after Dad, anxious lest I should be left behind in the swarming sweating crowd. Dad entered the fray, and began to haggle with the porters who had shouldered our bags (without the least idea of asking whether we wanted their services), and were aggressively negotiating payment before they even knew where we were headed!

A crowd of young children materialized screaming, "Baksheesh! Baksheesh!" grabbing at our arms and our clothing and miming hunger in hopes of getting a few piasters. I tried to shrug them off, and edged closer to Dad, who was trying to herd the victorious porters toward a taxi station, where the next stage of the battle would ensue as the disembarking passengers from the steamer fought for empty taxis. Several times he reached for the door handle of a parked vehicle, only to have someone stuff a suitcase through the open window on the other side, and the taxi lurch away, the smiling driver waving out the window and yelling "Malish! Malish!" (the Arabic equivalent of never mind).

Dad instructed us to guard the baggage from the hordes of children, who were still reveling in the general chaos, trying to pick our pockets or nab a small suitcase, in addition to the continually howling for Bakasheeh! Dad, generally a gentle and introverted person, periodically turned to yell "Imshee, imshee men henna!" but they were used to being screamed at, and continued to hassle until we all began to shout "Imshee!(go away!)." Finally, Dad cornered a policeman, who shook his stick at the children, scattering them, and located a taxi for us. We heaved our suitcases into the trunk and scrambled into the rickety vehicle as fast as we could. Anything to avoid another onslaught of young and accomplished beggars!

Perched on the edge of the seat between Ed and B. Jean, I breathed a sigh of relief. Too soon ... With a jerk that nearly landed me on the floor, the car came to life, and we were off on a trip which, in this country, people would have to pay for in an amusement park!

We plunged into the stream of traffic, forcing cars on either side to jostle for position. At one point we were actually off the road, driving down the sidewalk! The honking was incessant, every driver literally leaning on his horn with one hand and with the other shaking his fist out the window at anyone who got in his way. Donkey carts rattled by and bicycle bells rang. The air was blue with blazing curses. I wanted to hold my ears and hold my head, but I couldn't tear my eyes from the bicyclists weaving in and out of the mass, sliding through incredibly small spaces, one hand on their bells and the other reaching up to balance huge trays of bread or produce on their heads.

Pedestrians nearly outnumbered the assorted vehicles. They gathered in groups at the edge of the street, until they accumulated enough sheer mass to stop the traffic, and then surged across en masse, oblivious to hurled insults and shrieking brakes. It was with a sense of great relief that I heard Ed say, "There's the train station." And then, "Oh, no! Here we go again!" I thought, as the taxi stopped and I opened the car door, entering a new riot zone, with a fresh group of porters and the inevitable band of beggar children yelling for baksheesh.

When we had finally struggled onto the train and hoisted our bags up onto the luggage shelves, we fell into the seats exhausted. But there was no respite. Without a first class ticket, we were relegated to the back of the train, where the less well-off passengers were busily staking out territory, surrounded by wailing children, squawking chickens, and the strangest assortment of baggage and bundles of worldly goods that I had ever seen! It was a long, long ride to Khartoum.

When the puffing train finally labored into the station, Uncle Bill Philips was there to meet us. Thankfully, he had come in the mission vehicle, so the trauma of another taxi ride was averted. Even so, it was clear that driving defensively had a meaning all its own, as it does in many third world countries. The traffic was even worse than that in Kosti, and although Uncle Bill was perhaps the only driver who was not learning out his window to curse those in his way, I had the distinct feeling that he would have liked to. When we finally turned into the mission compound, and the gate clanged shut against the din that flung itself up from the streets, I sagged back against the seats, suddenly aware of how taut I had become. Whew! At least I was now in semi-familiar territory, since every time we entered or left the Sudan, we paused at least overnight at this mission station in the Sudanese capital.

Through the next several days, as I walked with Dad around the shops, looking for items Mom had asked for, that were not available in the south, I began to see Khartoum through different eyes. The flat-roofed buildings seemed to shimmer in the mist of red dust that clung to everything. All along the streets, shop owners stood by their wide-open doors, where colorful displays of wares tumbled out onto the sidewalk. A show of interest on our part often brought forth an invitation to tea in the back room, or for pungent Turkish coffee, the aroma of which permeated the entire shop. Everywhere, men in galabias and turbans smiled and nodded, and tried to entice us to their shops to haggle over prices.

My favorite time was toward evening, when the dust settled a little, and the traffic no longer strangled the streets. Then I was moved by the haunting call of the muezzin as it floated down from the minarets of the mosques, calling all the faithful to prayer. It seemed like a blessing of peace as everything slowed to a stop, and people everywhere knelt reverently where they were, bowed toward the holy city of Mecca, and prayed.

This was a different, softer city, in sharp contrast to the jaunty, jangling jungle of the daytime. Dusk blurred the glaring brittleness of the atmosphere, and the exquisitely polite side of the northern Sudanese was on display as they sauntered through the streets, or congregated for impromptu feasts around the wagon of a street vendor. Shish kabob and kufta sizzled over portable braziers, tantalizing our taste buds with the heavenly aroma of grilling lamb. Or, the wagon might have tameeya (felafel) frying to a wonderful golden crispness, with a flavor of dill, garlic and lemon that I have never been able to duplicate here in the States, though I had tried and tried.

What a delightful memory! Dad and Ed and I strolling through the evening softened streets looking for the tameeya with the largest following (and therefore the choicest product), and waiting impatiently in line to receive our portion, served in rolled up newspaper. How I wished it could always be so, wandering through the dusky warmth, eating tameeyas, and holding my father's hand.

But no. Our visas to Egypt came through, and Dad prepared to return to the Sudan, while we re-packed to continue on to Schutz. Uncle Bill took us to the train station to see Dad off, and there the finality of parting from my family began to sink in. As he gave me one last hug, I stood rocking back and forth, unable to respond, my throat tight with fear, love and abandonment. Unable to watch, or wave, I heard the whistle and hiss of the steam as the train pulled away, heading south, and taking my heart with it.

Little by little in those first weeks, I ventured out of my shell, like an uncertain turtle, vulnerable, and ready to withdraw at any moment. The school compound was full of fascinating things. There were tall, elegant date palms, up the trunks of which young Arab boys scuttled like so many monkeys, to pick the moist rich fruit. I surreptitiously tried it myself, but never achieved a height of more than a few feet up the scabby trunks.

The grape arbor was another attraction. Its brilliant white lattice was a bright contrast to the deep satiny green of the vines. I loved the shadowy patterns that played about underneath them when the sun was high. To my great embarrassment, I was caught wandering there by a sixth grade boy, who kissed me soundly and ran off yelling, "Don't you know that's Lover's Lane?" I hadn't known, and rubbed my cheek in amazement, not likely from then on to forget.

Most of all, I loved the little islands of manicured lawn that were scattered over the compound. Several of them sported rainbow-hued flowerbeds full of sweet peas and snapdragons. I had never seen either flower before, and spent many magical moments kneeling in the grass, snapping the tiny dragon flowers.

At morning recess, I discovered halvah, a Middle Eastern candy made of honey and sesame seeds. Oh what a taste! My mouth still waters at the thought. When I lined up for snacks every morning, I was in a fever of impatience. Would there be enough halvah, or would I have to settle for white goat cheese? Abdu and Abraheem, Egyptian men who worked in the kitchen, soon learned that I was decidedly crestfallen if they were out of halvah, and began to tease me by pretending that it was gone. This soon led to a conspiracy in which they would signal each other to run to the kitchen and get more for me when the supply on hand truly had run out. They nicknamed me, Halvah, and to my delight, they immediately called me that fifteen years later, when I returned to Schutz for a nostalgic visit.

By the middle of October, I began to feel that I was truly a part of the microcosm of American society that Schutz had created within the compound walls that separated us from the slums of Alexandria. There were kids of all ages, bonded together by the common experience of missionary life and separation from home. A close-knit feeling of community developed, which I have never experienced since, and for which I still occasionally mourn. Surrounded by this cocoon of acceptance, I began to reach past my own defenses, and develop friendships.

After supper, and before bedtime, was often the highlight of the day. The older kids, who would shortly be incarcerated in mandatory study hall, would join in the fun outside, where huge group games of Capture the Flag and Kick the Can would ensue. Rustling through the bushes, sneaking around corners like amateur crooks, we gave ourselves up to the excitement of the chase, and the compound was filled with jungle-like sounds, and shouts of triumph and despair. Sometimes more than half of the eighty boarding students would be spread over the grounds, down behind the tennis courts and even up on the roof of the maintenance building. I never cared who won or lost, I just wanted to be a part of it all. It was almost like being a part of a family again. Poor substitute that it was, sometimes it was almost enough.

Chapter Twelve: 1956

When it was over, everything we did was dated in relation to it. Before the evacuation, the year of the evacuation, after the evacuation …

We had been at Schutz for about two months, with seven long months to go until we would go home to the Sudan for the summer, and I was still spending many nights at Becky's bedside, feeling lonely and homesick. Self-absorbed, I was totally unaware of the political situation building in Egypt in 1956. The Arabs and the Israelis had been enemies for centuries, but as Israel sought to become a country in its own right, and the US seemed supportive, a feeling took root in the Arab countries, of which Egypt was a leader, that Americans were taking Israel's side. A violent and anti-American mood began to simmer.

Being only in the fourth grade, I hardly knew there was a place called Israel, other than the biblical one, and would have had difficulty locating it on a map in any case, because the Egyptian government censored all of our text books, and systematically blacked Israel out on the maps and in the text. In later years they even went so far as to censor the song from *My Fair Lady* which says, "the Hebrews say it backwards, which is really rather frightening …" When war broke out between the two countries, and Israel began to bomb the Suez Canal, as well as other strategic spots in Egypt, I was totally shocked and confused!

It was the day after Halloween, and we were in the middle of our second hour classes. I was daydreaming of the haunted house the night before, and of Pete and Jack fighting over who would be my partner, when suddenly the bell rang, and we were told to go to chapel. Chapel!? Now!? As I followed my classmates, I wondered what the special celebration was. Mr. Meloy looked deadly serious as he began talking about an evacuation. What did he mean? Slowly it began to dawn on me that he was telling us to go and pack all of our things and get ready to leave! Leave? Why? Where were we going? Questions flew, but he had no clear answers. "Just go and pack," he said. I was stunned! I could not grasp why we should be leaving, and worse yet, had not a clue as to where we were going!

Unsure what to do, I followed the lead of the older kids. Staring at my open suitcase, I tried to sort out what was happening. "Miss Murdoch said we were going to Italy," said Margie Roy (Italy! How would we get there, who would take care of us?), "or maybe the States?"

"Oh, I hope it's the States!" said Penny Pollack (faded faces from family photographs of aunts and uncles I barely knew, our house in Berkley, California, when I was four years old, that was the States to me). Fighting rising panic, I began to throw things into the suitcase.

"Naples is nice," Margie was saying. "We went there two years ago." I choked. It sounded like Timbuktu to me!

Miss Murdock appeared in the doorway. "Now listen girls," she said, "we've decided to try to send all the Sudan kids home." They say there are still trains running from Cairo, but we've got to hurry! (Home? Did she say we were going home?)

"Home?" I stammered.

"Yes," said Margie. "They must not have bombed the train station yet."

"Bombed!" I squeaked.

"The Israelis are bombing Egypt, silly. Now hurry up! Here, let me help you." She emptied my drawers into my suitcase, and shut it quickly. "Come on B. Jean, come on Kathy!"

I grabbed the suitcase and struggled down the stairs after her. At the boy's floor I met Ed. "We're going home!" we said in unison, as we hustled down to the waiting microbus, and squeezed in beside the other Sudani kids. "Why is Israel bombing us?" I whispered to Ed. He shrugged, "The Israelis have always hated the Egyptians." Enough to bomb them? My mind screamed. Everyone was caught up in the somber and uncertain mood, though it was tinged with the excitement of going home.

Toward evening, as we approached Cairo, the oppressive feeling of a nation at war, frightened and vulnerable, began to seep into us. It was close to dusk. We pulled up to the Girl's College, which was run by the American Mission, and were told that no trains would be heading south until morning, so we were parceled out to various families living in Cairo. As Ed and I were introduced to a young couple at the Girl's School, sirens began to wail. Lights all over the city, suddenly went out, and as darkness covered the streets, our host began to pull black curtains over the windows to shut out any tell-tale light. I blinked in the darkness, and then the scene was suddenly lit with a bizarre, acid light.

"What was that?" I stuttered.

"Bombs are dropping over the airport," our host replied, with a forced calm.

We were taken to the kitchen, where a lone candle burned. I tried to put on my best company manners as supper was served, but the candlelight seemed sinister, and the periodic blasting of the air raid siren made conversation impossible. Chaotic noises from the street filtered in through the curtains. People were cursing loudly at cars whose drivers persisted in using headlights, and even at a nervous smoker lighting up. Allah's name seemed to be on everyone's lips. "In sha Allah," God willing, we will get through this. I added my own fervent prayers for safety, and for one last train going south. Somehow, the night passed.

Early the next morning, we were all assembled at the train station, which had so far escaped obliteration. The word was that a few trains were still running south to Assuit. Tickets had been purchased, but as usual, that did not guarantee a seat! We shoved and pummeled in a truly Arab manner, terrified that we would be left behind! At last, stuffed between bundles of pungent clothing, baskets of food with much the same order, squawking chickens and screaming children, we were on the train, going home!

When the train pulled safely out of the Cairo station, we began to relax a little. Everything began to seem more normal as we chugged along through the fertile crescent of Lower Egypt. The fellaheen farmers in the fields we passed seemed to be going about their daily routines, unaware of the war machine in motion over the capital city. A sort of holiday spirit began to effervesce, and soon we were singing old camp songs, and telling stories of life on the various stations in the South Sudan, celebrating our early release from school and the unexpected vacation ahead!

Eventually, we succumbed to fatigue, and snored fitfully through the last hours of the trip, to arrive that night in Assuit, in the middle of a blackout. We stumbled from the train, dragging suitcases we hoped were ours, and crowding together on the platform. No one was there to meet us, due to the blackout, and there was no way to get to the Assuit school compound until it lifted. I perched on my suitcase, trying to make out familiar faces. Jack materialized beside me and said, "Come on Kathy, let's sing." He had a ukulele he was learning to plunk out tunes on, so as we waited for the all clear to sound, we raised our voices in the great old hymns, "Onward Christian Soldiers ..."

Staff from the mission school eventually joined us at the station, and managed to herd us all into vehicles that took us to the school, where we bedded down for the night. A day or so later, we went on to Luxor, to catch the steamer heading south. By this time, I was enjoying myself thoroughly. I had no idea that there was a good chance the border between Egypt and the Sudan would be closed when we got there.

As we divided up to fill the fleet of taxis, there was Jack at my elbow again! I blushed, remembering again the trip through the haunted house at Schutz, which now seemed eons ago, but then gave myself up to enjoying the attention. As the caravan of taxis and mission cars began the long trek across the desert, excitement began to wane. We seemed to crawl along, delayed by flat tires and deflated by the sweltering heat. Our canteens were nearly empty, and we were close to comatose by the time we arrived.

When we arrived, the activity was suddenly frantic! The steamer was set to leave at any moment. Rumors that the border would close were heard on all sides. Dr. Reed and his wife hurried us through customs, and haggled with the officials to make sure that there was a berth for everyone. I was the last one through, only to hear the customs man exclaim: "Kafia! Enough! There is no more room!" My face crumpled in horror, but Mrs. Reed took me under her wing, soothingly telling me that it would be OK, they would not leave me behind. I buried my face gratefully in her bosom, and did so again for the next four nights as I shared her bunk. There had indeed been no more room!

Our arrival in Malakal occasioned quite a celebration! Our parents had had only intermittent bits of news as to where we were, and what the current plan was. Understanding the political situation, and gathering what news they could as the Suez crisis escalated they had spent the week plagued with worry and fear for our safety. But we were home! Home early that first year at Schutz, the Year of the Evacuation.

Chapter Thirteen: Nya mun a dubo

I woke suddenly, glanced around, and pinched myself to be sure it was true. I really was out on the sleeping porch! That really was Gwen beside me! I really was at Dolieb Hill! I was home!

The next few months were heaven. Not only was I back home. Friends from school were there also. Looking back, I'm not sure what possessed my mother to agree to keep three children from other mission families and include them in our daily school routine. Teaching was certainly not her favorite task, and adding three children to her own four was a courageous move. We made quite a lively student body. Jack and Peter were in Ed's class, and B. Jean was in mine. The two boys actually lived with us, and B. Jean came in daily, as her family lived in Malakal.

Everything we did seemed so much more exciting with peers to join us. Climbing to the tree house, sneaking through the house howling, "Ayoop! Ayoop!" as we pretended to be hyenas, digging wonderful tunnels in the enormous sand pile that had been hauled in to mix concrete for a new building, and yes, even studying, took on a new luster. I didn't even mind when the boys insisted on going off alone to fish, as long as they included the rest of us in the feast. Nor did it matter that the fish were invariably tiny. We would gather around a small stick fire and feast on roasted minnows, savoring every charred bite, as if it were silky black caviar.

One day the oppressiveness of the dry season heat was suddenly broken by insistent clapping at the back door, and cries of "Oshoda! Oshoda!" On the nearby sleeping porch heads of supposedly napping children bobbed up, and eyes began to glisten. Something was afoot!

The schoolboy's black skin was sheened in sweat and he stumbled over his words in his excitement. We strained to catch familiar words from the rapid conversation. Other schoolboys were beginning to cluster around, and then we saw Dad point to the river, and a word we recognized was on all lips. Nyang- Crocodile!

I shrugged my shoulders, trying to dislodge the prickles of fear. I remembered the Sunday service held down by the river not long ago. Dad had stepped into the water to baptize a new convert when suddenly chaos erupted on the bank! The familiar ripples of a crocodile snout breaking the water had been sighted! I don't think the issue of baptism by immersion vs. baptism by sprinkling has ever been so quickly settled!

The native people feared the crocodile. Not only were they an obvious danger to cattle, and children bathing in the river, the native belief in reincarnation and evil spirits endowed them with supernatural powers. Stories of Nya mun a dubo coming out of the river and devouring entire villages added to the fear and superstition that the crocodile inspired.

In spite of, or perhaps because of, the spiritual miasma surrounding the crocodile, the hide was highly valued for use as a shield, and its possession conferred great status on the owner. Because of this, the native men did occasionally attempt to kill them, but being armed only with a primitive spear, it was a dangerous enterprise. When the missionaries arrived with their guns, the people often preferred to call on them rather than hunt down crocodiles themselves.

So, Dad loaded his rifle and headed for the river, followed by a group of gibbering schoolboys. We poured out of the house and joined the cavalcade, and on arriving at the riverbank stationed ourselves among the tall bamboo. Somehow the leafy bower seemed to offer a little protection, and we huddled down, pushing aside the leaves to peer out at the river.

All eyes were scanning the water for the tell-tale trail of the crocodile snout breaking the surface. I raised my arm to point, just as the gun exploded beside me and the crocodile flew several feet into the air! "Ya par mal one meter long," screamed one schoolboy, so astonished that he mixed his native Shilluk with the English he was learning. There was a general hubbub on the shore as the obviously injured animal thrashed around and bellowed in pain.

Some of the older boys climbed into the dugout canoe and rowed out to where the normally slow moving river had virtually become a whirlpool! Through my bamboo barrier, I watched them glide closer and closer to the spot where the crocodile had disappeared, spears at the ready. The next instant the croc leaped into the air and the nearly upset the advancing canoe. The entire end of its nose looked mangled and raw! I swallowed a shriek, screwed my eyes shut, and held my breath, waiting for the final shot. It never came.

Slowly opening my eyes, I saw the schoolboys fanning out along the riverbank, loudly exclaiming about the freak shot, and the fact that the crocodile had gotten away. As the noise of the search receded into the distance, so did my courage. In my imagination, the crocodile hid underneath the floating waves, viciously plotting its revenge. I ripped through the bamboo, which suddenly seemed to confine, rather than protect me, and tore up the hill, followed by the others, who professed nonchalance, but were not far behind.

Several days later, a young schoolboy again came to clap at the door, asking for Oshoda. The crocodile was down by his village, he said. They could smell its rotting flesh and hear it snorting in the grass as it tried to breathe through its mutilated nose. No one in the village dared go near it, afraid that in its wounded condition it would be more dangerous than ever.

With some misgiving, I piled into the back of the Land Rover with everyone else, including the schoolboy. And Dad headed for the village. As we approached, the outlines of tukles and kaals took shape against the horizon. The heavy scent of danger and fear was palpable. The entire village had been pushed to the edge of insanity by fear of the wounded animal. Even the little naked children were cowering in the doorways.

It was getting hot. Dry grassland stretched for miles, interrupted occasionally by a scrubby thorn tree. The only green to be seen was right along the river, where the crocodile was holed up. I became aware of a stifling stench oozing up off the water, and noticed vultures circling above, waiting for the death knell of the wounded croc. As we pulled up by the river, we could hear the snuffling snort of the crocodile's labored breathing.

I watched breathlessly as Dad stalked through the grass. Suddenly it parted violently, and the infuriated reptile rushed out, thrashing its huge tail and roaring its torment. Frantically it charged the circle of native men armed with spears. Blinded by rage and pain, it was unsure which one was its enemy. The gunshot burst through the confusion, and there was sudden calm. The croc thrashed fitfully for a few more seconds, and lay still.

Shouts of warning turned into chants of relief as the villagers spontaneously erupted with praise for Oshoda and his gun.

"We are saved! Oshoda had killed the Nya muna dubo. The gun has overcome the spirit of the river!"

Chapter Fourteen: Lover's Lane

My career as a Schutzite reached its height during my second year. No longer plagued by homesickness, I was able to relax and began to really enjoy myself. Morn's letters to her own mother at that time report that I wrote nearly every week about how happy I was, and what fun I was having. I suspect that I did not reveal the nature of many of the fun times, since I quite often skirted the rules, and got great satisfaction out of not getting caught (or at least not often). The list of regulations seemed to me not only endless but tiresome; get up with the rising bell, go to work crew, don't be late to breakfast, pay attention in class, get homework done, don't talk in study hall, watch your table manners, clean your room for inspection, stay off the boy's floor, lights out at 8:00, etc., etc., etc.

At one level I was a model student, never openly rebellious, always polite and cooperative with those in charge, at least on the surface. The challenge was in deciding which rules were made to be broken, and then convincing my peers to go along with the plan. I would not have dreamed of going down to the boy's floor, for example, but I saw no reason why that should keep me from talking to the boys after lights out. Every floor of the dormitory building had a balcony, one above the other, so all we had to do was get the boys to come out onto their balcony while we were on the one above.

When we discovered that the little canteen we frequented just outside the compound gate had little whistles, we were ecstatic! Every night thereafter, when the housemother had made her rounds, we would step onto the balcony and tweet the prearranged signal. Afraid that actual talking would alert someone, we ran a string with a little box tied to it from our balcony down to the boys, and by such means I received my first love letters.

Too young to date, my friends and I devised not so subtle means of showing that we were attracted to someone. Accidentally on purpose getting caught in Lover's Lane was the ideal, but there was a risk of misjudging timing, and getting caught by the wrong person! Boy catch girl tag was another favorite, but again it required knowing when to run like the wind, and when to only pretend.

Those in my age group were fascinated by the older kids who could actually date. Unfortunate couples were constantly harassed by catcalls from the branches of trees that grew near Lover's Lane. They were subjected to snorts and snickers whenever they sought each other out at mealtime or study hall, and often developed mild paranoia, for just as they thought they were alone, a movement in the bushes, or a whispered taunt would alert them. Privacy was at a premium for all persecuted duos, their search for it constantly frustrated by youngsters who secretly longed to trade places.

The flat roof of the dormitory building, where laundry was strung out to dry by the washer women, and the ironing man sweated, knee deep in piles of wrinkled clothing, was a favorite meeting place for an evening tete a tete. The first challenge was to get there without being observed, since the only access was up the main stairway, which connected all the floors and led all the way up to the door that opened onto the roof.

One night as I crossed the landing of the stairway, I noticed that one of the high school boys, Glenn, was headed for the roof. I slid behind the door to the east wing and waited. Several seconds elapsed, and then Pam peered out onto the landing from the opposite wing. I shrank back. Satisfied that no one was about, she dashed up the stairs after Glenn, and I ran to get Becky. "Come on!" I whispered, jerking my head toward the door. "Glenn and Pam are on the roof!"

Furtively we slunk through the hallway, trying not to look too conspicuous. Taking the first flight of stairs as normally as possible, we slid around the landing and began to tiptoe up the last stretch. The door out to the roof was open, revealing total darkness as we reached the top step. All was still, and we paused to stifle nervous giggles. As we eased towards the door, a hoarse voice grated out, "Someone's coming!" Frantically we scrambled back behind the door, barely escaping Glenn as he stumbled onto the lighted stairway.

I held my breath, not daring to look at Becky. What if he saw us? Trying vainly to think of some excuse for being where we were, and knowing that he would not believe me, I stuffed my hand in my mouth to quiet my breathing and prayed for invisibility. We heard Glenn returning up the stairs, muttering to himself as he passed us by. Then all was still. So far, so good! Becky was looking wide-eyed and signaling retreat, but I was thrilled by the close call, and ready to go on. I stole through the doorway, into the darkness, and felt Becky close behind me.

We flattened ourselves against the wall of the ironing room, and inched along, stopping to listen and peer through the blackness. Nothing. Frustrated, I stopped suddenly, and an involuntary "oh" escaped as Becky bumped into me.

"Darn it! Someone is up here," Glenn muttered. "I'll catch them this time!" He sounded dreadfully close, and definitely angry! Grabbing Becky's hand, I raced along the wall, through the door to the ironing room, and dived under the closest mound of dirty sheets. We heard Glenn's footsteps at the door. His heavy breathing seemed to be coming from right above us as we cowered under cover.

"If I ever catch whoever you are, you'll be sorry!" he yelled. I didn't doubt it. I was sorry already! Expecting any moment to have my sheets yanked off, I tried to burrow further in, but that must have been his parting shot, for we heard retreating footsteps, and then silence.

"I think he's gone," I whispered.

"I hope so," said Becky, "but how are we going to get out of here?" That gave me pause. How indeed? Glenn was very likely lurking on the stairs, knowing that we would have to come out sooner or later.

Suddenly the shrill sound of the bedtime bell blasted from the ringer just above us, and I buried my face in the sheets that had saved us, trying to stem the flood of hysterical giggles that was rising like a shaken soda in my throat. "They'll have to go in now," I choked. "We're saved by the bell!"

Chapter Fifteen: Across the Sahara

"It's not so nice being away from our mothers and fathers, but we do have adventures," Chloe explained to our chaperon. I was thoroughly in agreement. Going back to Schutz after summer vacation meant re-uniting with friends, as well as the resumption of old animosities and a hope for a new romance. Scary yet exciting.

In 1959 one of Uncle Lowrie's daughters, Ruth, escorted 25 missionary children from the South Sudan up to Schutz. For several days children trickled into Malakal from outlying stations, most flying in on MAF, the Missionary Aviation Fellowhip, which was based in Malakal and had several pilots and small Cessna Aircraft that flew to all the stations, delivering needed supplies and mail, picking up patients that needed care at the government hospital, and providing whatever other services they could to keep missionaries in the out-posts connected with semi-civilization.

Since we lived only about seventeen miles from Malakal, we didn't often use the MAF services. This was a source of aggravation for me, because I had a crush on one of the pilots, and I was also dying to see what it was like to land and take off from the river in the pontoon plane. Once, several years into junior high, we did get to do this. It was just as thrilling as I had hoped. The memory of zooming down the river, faster than I had ever gone, with huge waves of water pouring past the windows on both sides of the plane, still evokes the exhilaration that I felt then. No amusement park ride has ever matched it.

But, in 1959, Dad took us to Malakal by boat. By we, I mean Dad and the four of us kids. This was the first year that all four of us were going to Schutz. Mom had been dreading it for some time, as had Tim, who was only in the third grade. We left Mom at Dolieb Hill, where, unknown to us, she was hiding in the attic, sobbing her heart out. How terribly terribly hard to leave your children in someone else's care for nine months! Now, a mother myself, I cannot imagine how she was able to do it. I'm not sure that Dad's feelings were any less intense than were Mom's, but he kept all of that from us, and we never knew what private grief he was holding back behind his calm exterior.

By the time we got to Malakal, the guest house there was overflowing with children of all ages and stages of development, from third graders like Tim, clear up to seniors in high school. Shortly after we joined the crowd, everyone was packed into all available vehicles to go to the little tarmac that passed for an airport. There the lengthy weighing in began. One by one, in front of God and everyone, we had to step on the scales and have our weight recorded. I was, by now, about twelve years old, and not yet terribly weight conscious, but in the next few years, the embarrassment of everyone knowing what I weighed was an annual torture.

When all of us, and then all of our baggage had been weighed, everything was loaded onto the Dakota airplane, we hugged and kissed Dad one last time and packed ourselves into the tiny plane, ready for the bumpy flight to Khartoum. The engines revved, the plane shook somewhat alarmingly, and we were off!

Tim was stuck in the last seat, with Ruth for a seatmate. Before we had been aloft more than a few minutes, he told her, most politely, that his eyes were tired from nothing to look at, and could he please go and sit with Ronnie. She very helpfully arranged a transfer.

A little later, trying to pass the time, Ruth began to banter with the older girls, speculating as to whether there were enough parachutes aboard for all of us, should the plane crash. "Oh, we won't need parachutes, we prayed," one of the younger kids reported blithely. I wished I felt that secure. The old Dakota bucked and creaked as it wrestled with the hot desert air, making my stomach lurch alarmingly. Reaching for an air sickness bag, I was horrified to find that there were none in the pocket where they should be. "Call the stewardess," I muttered to B. Jean, "I'm going to throw up!" She complied, leaning as far away from me as she could get. It was no good. Just as the stewardess arrived with a newspaper rolled into a cone for my use, I lost control and spewed nasty yellow vomit over both of our laps!

Mercifully, we finally arrived at Khartoum. Deplaning, we were assaulted by a predictably furnace-like blast of the dry desert wind. Looking back, one of the clearest memories I have of Khartoum is standing in the doorway of a plane, facing heat that seemed to rise like fog off the tarmac, and struggling to inflate my flattened lungs before lunging down the stairway and into the confusion of the airport. It was an experience often repeated over the years.

When we reached the American Mission Compound that afternoon, it was like a mini-reunion. Mission kids whose families were in Ethiopia, Cameroon, and other countries of the southern part of the continent were already there, waiting for us to join them on the final leg of the journey to Alexandria, and Schutz. There were children everywhere, walking along the top of the compound wall, protruding from the branches of trees, and even exploring the roofs of some of the lower buildings. Before long some of the boys, led by female-hating Billy, had created a "girl net" from an old blanket, and were setting out to see who they could snare. The girls, naturally, took up the challenge and ran screaming into the bedrooms, looking for a "boy net." For the next few hours there was pandemonium. By evening, we were all emotionally and physically exhausted, and able to slip into sleep, with homesickness only a vague presence at the edges of consciousness.

Chapter Sixteen: Shall We Dance?

"Allemande left with your left hand, pass your partner, right and left grand ..." My toes were tapping before I ever got out to the basketball court, which was already awhirl with lovely full skirts do-se-doing and swinging in time to the catchy country rhythm. I had on my brand new square dance skirt of gray and pink tiers with rickrack around the edges, and felt like a Spanish flamenco dancer. How gloriously it twirled and swirled around my legs when my partner swung me round! "Stick out slips" were the rage at Schutz then. Starched multi layers of netting that poufed the skirt out, and swished wonderfully with each dance movement. I always felt gorgeous in that outfit!

I was somewhat amazed to discover, in the sixth grade, that I could dance. I was never particularly athletic, or in kinesthetic tune with my body, as Dad, Tim and Gwen were. But, I could dance, and I could do it well! It was such a thrill to get a good partner, who could swing me nearly off my feet, catching the rhythm, just as I did, so that every move was smooth and flowing, even in the most intricate patterns. Tim was one of the best partners I ever had when he grew taller and stronger than I was, and we often danced a set or two together just for the thrill of it.

One year, we organized a square dance team, and put together a performance of some of the more difficult routines. I was in heaven! Not only did I get to dance more often, but my current crush, Mike Dillon, was my partner!

I fell in and out of crushes easily, and usually secretly, since I lacked the self-confidence to let a guy know that I liked him. The older I got, the more difficult it seemed for me to feel at ease with the opposite sex. Though I had girlfriends, who told me that the guys would really like me if only I could think of something to say to them, I could not seem to master the art.

So, I kept my crushes secret. Or so I thought. When Tim and Mom and I went to the big Schutz celebration in 1999, I was thrilled to see that Mike Dillon was going to be there! "I don't suppose I should tell him what a crush I had on him," I said to Tim. "I certainly don't want to know who had a crush on me," he replied.

When I came face to face with Mike, I never would have known him. He had turned into a huge, white haired Texan, proud proprietor of a Bed and Breakfast near Austin. He had come to the reunion accompanied by his wife and two teenaged daughters, but he still gave me a big bear hug, and before I knew it, words I never meant to say were flying out of my mouth. "I shouldn't embarrass you in front of your family, but I was absolutely crazy about you when we were on the square dance team," I blurted. He grinned as big as Texas, and said, "I know!" at which point I fled the scene, laughing at myself, still speechless in the presence of a guy I liked!

For most of the time that I was at Schutz, square dancing was the only form of dancing that was allowed, due to the conservative religious outlook of most of the missionary parents of the boarding population. We did take ballet lessons one year, and even gave a performance of sorts, but by and large only square dancing was allowed. Since I had never been exposed to anything else, and since it was something I loved, I was never bothered, except for the last two years I was there, when the dances became less frequent, and attendance fell off dramatically. The atmosphere at Schutz was changing, and I really didn't want to change with it.

My senior year was the first time I attended a party where anything other than square dancing was done. There was a large influx of day students that year. These were kids whose parents worked for the American embassy in Egypt or were connected with Shell Oil Co, which did much business in Egypt. Most of them had spent much more time in the States than those of us who were missionary kids, and they brought different values and cultural expectations with them. My memory is no longer clear as to who arranged the dancing party, or where it was held, though I am sure it was not on the Schutz compound.

Although I attended the party full of trepidation, I had sewn for myself a bright red straight-line skirt, which I felt was very stylish. I was determined to be "in vogue" and to try something new. The twist was just becoming popular, so twist and shout I did!

Slow dancing, however, turned my feet to wooden blocks, which weighed a ton, and reduced my movement to an uncoordinated shuffle. I was so tense that I almost literally turned to stone. I think that the proximity of a male partner stopped more than just my heart. It was many many years before I overcame my fears and took a dance class with a friend of mine. What a thrill to discover that I could dance the waltz, the fox trot, the tango (well, maybe not the tango). When I moved to St Louis I found, to my delight, that there were country-dance groups, and once again I could join a group of people who loved to allemande left …

Chapter Seventeen: Land of the Pharaohs

In 1999 a huge gathering of former Schutzites, some of whom were there when the school was first opened, was held to celebrate the 75th birthday of Schutz. My brother Tim, my mother, and I went. It was a weekend of wonderful reminiscing!

During my parents' reign as houseparents at Schutz, I was too self-absorbed to realize that their presence might affect anyone besides myself. Therefore, I was somewhat amazed by the response of so many who were Schutzites during my time there, when they greeted my mother. Over and over during that weekend, people told me what a wonderful presence she holds in their memories.

At one point Mom and I were waiting for a program to start, looking around, identifying various people and commenting on what they were doing now, thirty years later. A man about my age, seated in front of us, turned around, looked at my name tag, and said, "Kathy Adair!" I nodded, trying to place his face. Perhaps he had been one of the "little kids" when I had moved on to the upper echelons and become one of the "big kids?"

"Are you related to Martha Adair?" he asked me.

"She's my mother," I said, gesturing to her sitting beside me. He jumped up from his chair and flung his arms around her crying, "Aunt Martha!" A little stunned, she craned her neck to try to get a glimpse of his name tag.

"Oh, you don't know me," he said. "I came the year after you left, and all I ever heard about was Aunt Martha and Uncle Bill. I was so jealous of all the kids who had you for house parents, because they had such great times when you were there! No one liked the couple that came after you left. They were so mean! We all refused to call them aunt and uncle, even though we were told to." What a lovely and unexpected tribute to the legacy my parents gave to many Schutzites.

One of the most amazing experiences of the reunion for me, was going to hear Dr. James Hoffmeir, a noted archeologist, talk about his most recent research related to the path the Israelites took out of Egypt, and their crossing of the Red, or perhaps the Reed, Sea. Jim was a crony of Tim's when they were in junior high and the leader of many a hilarious escapade. About six of the guys who were part of that clan attended the reunion. Oh the stories they told! My favorite was of Hoffmeir trying to light one of his farts with a match and catching his underwear on fire!

So, when Dr. Hoffmeir rose to speak, looking like a bushy, bearded, replica of his younger self, thanked Miss Bode for her introduction and said, "The first thing Miss Bode asked me was 'So, when did you grow up?'" the place broke up. Then we listened in astonishment, which turned to respect as he began to share with great knowledge and passion, about his research.

Jim mentioned in his talk several Boy Scout trips out to the desert, which my dad had organized, and the thrill he felt, even then, of finding ancient coins and arrowheads. There were widespread murmurs of agreement, as this was a common response of many Schutzites. But not for me. I frankly, at the time, could not have cared any less.

Even so, I was a little intrigued when my folks came up to Schutz one Christmas, and decided to take us to see some of the tourist attractions of ancient Egypt. We went first to Luxor, which is the modern incarnation of the ancient city of Thebes. We stayed at the mission guest house, and it is from there that my most potent memory of the whole trip came. Every morning for breakfast there were fragrant home baked rolls, and with these came thick clotted cream mixed with luscious orange marmalade. After thirty years my mouth still waters as I remember.

Thebes was where the famous temple of Karnak was built to honor Amon Re, the most important of the Egyptian gods. It was one of the great wonders of its time, large enough to hold several cathedrals! The hall of columns entering the area, known as the great hypostyle, still has remnants of its once impressive grandeur. Walking through the remains of the marvelous temple, I tried to imagine who must have walked there when it was gloriously new. What did it mean to them in the culture of that time? Did they stand in breathless wonder at the immensity of it all? Did those who saw it daily come to take it all for granted?

Ramses II, who is credited with building the hypostyle at Karnak, also built a spectacular rock temple at Abu Simble. Guarding the entrance to this temple are four gigantic statues of pharaoh, seated on a throne. Once again I was overcome by the sheer size of these stern carved figures. Although I don't recall visiting this site when we were little, Mom later showed me pictures of all four of us kids perched on one big toe!

It was this site that was flooded in the sixties when the Aswan Dam was completed. Knowing how massive these structures were, I was amazed to watch documentaries on TV showing how they were moved stone by stone and reassembled at another location to prevent their destruction when the lake formed behind the new dam. It was a challenge to modern technology, how did the ancient people ever, with primitive tools, manage to create them?

The Valley of the Kings, a huge necropolis, or city of the dead, holds the tombs of many of the ancient pharaohs. Although tomb robbers decimated much of the funereal wealth of these burial places, wall paintings describing the lives of those entombed there can still be seen. One of the most interesting of these tombs was that of Queen Hatshepsut, whose husband was pharaoh, and died, leaving his infant son the next in line to rule. The Queen was to serve as reagent until he attained his majority, but instead had herself declared pharaoh, and ruled for twenty years. Her tomb is a gorgeous temple, completely hewn from a solid stone mountainside. Climbing the numerous steps, gazing at the way the façade seemed to flow from the mountain, I wondered if Queen Hatshepsut had had a hand in the design, or was there a royal architect assigned, or perhaps some sort of contest to win the honor of creating this enduring beauty?

Clearer in my memory than any other sites we visited are the pyramids of Giza and the great Sphinx, just west of Cairo. When we were there, tourists were still allowed to climb to the top of the great pyramid, built by Khufu in about 2600 BC, so the four of us and Dad decided to try. We left Mom seated on a rock at the bottom of the pyramid, stating that she had no desire to make the climb. When we got back, she was wishing she had. No sooner had she settled down to wait than a huge commotion arose. She turned, and saw a herd of camels, and wildly gesticulating camel drivers headed straight for her! She hopped up on a rock just in time, and stood there shaking as they streaked past her on both sides!

The climb was not easy, since the average weight of the limestone blocks from which it is made is 2.5 tons, and some were large enough that we had to pull ourselves up over each edge. As we struggled toward the top, 481 feet in the air, we were left in the dust by several local Arabs who were racing to set the fastest time for a climb up and back.

Huffing and puffing, we finally clambered onto the top, and stood looking out over the Sphinx, on the edge of the great desert. How many slaves had died in the heat and sand as they struggled to build these structures, all for the comfort of the god-like pharaoh when he passed into the afterlife? What, I wondered, did the slaves themselves have to look forward to when they passed over. Would their existence there be an improvement over the lives they lived in their present?

All ancient Egyptians believed in the afterlife, and spent their earthly lives preparing for it. Perhaps it is this understanding that makes me feel some connection with these ancestors. Seeing life on earth as trial and preparation for the coming existence in the eternal realm, seems to me to be a thoroughly modern theme, and so now, I find that I do care about the ancients, and look for other lessons they can teach.

.

Chapter Eighteen: Wanglel

Summertime, when we were home from Schutz, was always a special time for us as a family. My mother would cut down the number of hours she spent working at the clinic so that she could be home with us, and, as she put it, "make memories." It's the most precious gift she ever gave us.

Picnics were a favorite memory-making activity. We also spent time visiting other mission families in Obel and Malakal, which were the stations closest to ours. Once, Mom found the script to an old melodrama, complete with villain and fair maiden. She assigned each of us a part, and when we had practiced, and practiced and practiced, we went to Malakal and performed for the missionaries there, who were quite undemanding, and gave us a standing ovation.

Several times, we visited stations that we had never been to before, or where there were no longer families assigned. Our trip to Wanglel was one of the more memorable of these. The station was established when work in the Sudan was expanded to tribes other than the Shilluk. The people in the Wanglel area are Nuers, another of the four major tribes of the Southern Sudan. My grandparents had been assigned there for some time when they were serving in the Sudan.

At the time of our visit to Wanglel, no mission families were assigned there. A government post had been established and maintained. The Nuer church thrived, operated by indigenous, mission-trained pastors.

The boat trip from Dolieb Hill to Wanglel covered about 45 miles. Down the Sobat about six miles to the Nile, 25 miles or so up the Nile and then 15 miles against the strong swift current of the Zeraf River. It took about six hours of chug-a-lugging along with two outboard motors and an overloaded sixteen-foot aluminum boat.

We arrived at Wanglel on a Saturday afternoon. By the time we had unloaded everything it was evening and the local mosquito horde was beginning to make itself felt. Slapping and scratching, we tried to settle in while Mom fixed supper over the kerosene stove we had brought. Eventually, we got the mosquito nets hung and dived under them for cover, where the irritating whine pursued us into sleep. It was a long night.

In the morning we had an early breakfast, and then Dad went off to Nuer church, and we held our own Sunday School before seeking out entertainment. I was an avid tree climber, so I wandered outside and soon found an inviting neem tree just outside the screened causeway that connected two parts of the building. Soon I was nestled among the leaves, happily daydreaming.

Suddenly, I was yanked back to reality by terrified screams coming from the causeway where Gwen and Tim were playing. Fearing snakes, or something worse, I scrambled from my arboreal retreat and ran. Through the screen door I saw Gwen, screaming in horror as she knelt by Tim who was lying face down in a pool of blood! Mom arrived on the scene and turned him over, wiping the blood on her skirt and trying to assess the damage. In short order she sent Ed to get Dad at the church and me to find what limited first aid supplies we had.

By the time Dad arrived, Mom was applying pressure as best she could, but the size of the cut above Tim's eye concerned her, and despite her best efforts, it continued to bleed. "This doesn't look good," she said to Dad. "It needs to be stitched, and I can't do that here. We need to get him to Dr. Doris in Obel as soon as possible."

Frightened, and feeling far from help, we threw everything into the boat as quickly as we could. Mom was afraid Tim would go into shock, so we fashioned a space where he could lie down, and took off. It was a long and frightening trip. I had never seen anyone in that much pain close up, and this was my little brother! He looked so pale and weak! What if he died? Surely God would not take Tim too!

Mom and Dad took turns steering the boat, the swiftness of the current helping us, now that we were headed back toward the Nile. As we poked along, we tried to keep our eyes on the water, on the lookout for signs of an old sunken boat, probably an Arab dhow that blocked part of the river and would cause considerable damage, not to mention wasting precious time, if we didn't see it in time.

Then, it began to rain, shrouding us all in a nasty cold veil that obscured the surface of the river, and set us all to shivering, as our concern for Tim increased. Every minute seemed like hours as we ploughed on and on, each sunk in our own dismal thoughts. At one point Mom was shaken out of her torpor by the sight of the long scaly snout of a crocodile, surfacing right beside the boat! Fortunately, it lost interest, and dove under the boat, back to its own pursuits.

When the three scrawny palms that marked the dock at Obel came into sight, we were so tired and cold and worried that we could hardly summon up the energy to disembark. Mom and Dad sent Ed and I to get Dr. Doris, while she and Dad lifted Tim, whose pulse was fluttering alarmingly, out of the boat and carried him up to the house.

Doris' husband Tal rushed to help, and soon Tim was lying on the dining room table, with Doris and Mom cleaning the gash on his forehead in preparation for stitching it up. This was more than I could stomach. I retreated to the other end of the verandah, covered my ears, and tried to concentrate on singing every hymn I knew.

Tal tried to distract everyone by pacing back and forth beside the makeshift operating table, reading aloud from a children's book, while

Dad sat beside Tim, holding his hand and trying to keep him still. Halfway through the procedure, Dr. Doris looked up and said, "Tal, you better catch Bill!" "Oh, we men are strong," Tal replied, and then turned to see Dad slide off his chair in a dead faint!

Tim wore his scar with some pride for a number of years before the whiteness faded. It was only the first of many, as even into adulthood, he continues to rush head long through life.

Chapter Nineteen: Fulfillment Papers

In 1963 the Sudanese government presented Mom and Dad, as well as all of the other missionaries still in the Sudan, with their Fulfillment Papers. In stilted Officialese, the document stated, "I have been directed to inform you that you should leave the Sudan within six weeks of this day... for the fulfillment of the object for which you have been allowed to enter the Sudan." One mission worker was told that they were a "dangerous group, and the Government could no longer tolerate your presence."

The arrival of these papers was not entirely unforeseen. For several years tension had been building, as the government in the predominantly Muslim North Sudan tried to exert more and more control over the Christian and Animist South. The roots of this conflict were deep in the history of the nation, dating back to an era where the light skinned northerners went to the south to take the black skinned southerners as slaves. To this day, the conflict has not been resolved, and over the years, the country has been destroying itself, a quietly developing tragedy, with as many human rights violations as have been seen in Rwanda. Because this country has nothing to offer the rest of the world, it has been allowed to slowly commit suicide.

Although the conflict began due to racial and cultural issues, in 1963 the Mahdists and the Muslim Brotherhood who were influential in the government, began to specifically target Christians as the enemy. They feared the solidarity which the common religion gave to its southern followers, and began to mark Christian leaders for arrest, harassment, and imprisonment. Many of those who were friends of my father were already in jail. Those who could, were leaving the country, to live in exile until it became safe to return.

The last few years that my parents spent in the Sudan were very difficult. Government control had gradually increased over the years. They took over the boys and girls schools that the mission had started, and began to dictate what could and could not be taught. The climate became more and more hostile as the government accused mission workers of anti-government activities and paid informers to provide false information. More than once Dad was taken to Malakal and brought before the police commissioner to be faced with blatant lies and threatened with expulsion.

Sometimes in earlier years we had been subjected to curfews, and there had been shooting and unrest in Malakal when the political situation was uneasy, especially when independence was declared from Britain. But, until these end times, missionaries had always been seen as benefactors, supporting, rather than threatening. Dad says that it was very difficult not to take things personally, and he and Mom often discussed leaving before the situation became dangerous. But he felt that the most important work of his mission career was the completion of the translation of the New Testament into the Shilluk language, and he could not abandon it.

Many mission families had already been expelled when Mom and Dad finally got their orders to leave. Other families had gone to Ethiopia to continue mission work in that country. Was that where they were also called to go? Could the translation work be continued outside the Sudan? If so, where? What would happen to the struggling Christian church after they left, and its leaders and followers were systematically imprisoned and tortured?

Outside the country voices were raised in protest. Bill Anderson (son of the senior missionary still in the Sudan at the time my parents were expelled) wrote to the "African Standard" of Nairobi, "As one who worked in the Sudan for a number of years, I would like to comment on the astonishing statement by the Sudanese Embassy defending the recent expulsion of missionaries. If the Sudan government justified its actions on the grounds that the missionaries were only guests in their country, with no inherent right to stay there, it might carry some conviction. What they are doing, however, is to place the main blame for the rebellion now raging throughout the South on several hundred 'politically minded' missionaries.

"At a time when, according to your own report, more than 5,000 African Sudanese have fled into Karamoja, such an accusation looks merely absurd. The tragic issue in the country is the terror faced by the entire population, whether Muslim, Christian or Pagan. Suspects have been arrested and savagely beaten and imprisoned. Whole villages suspected of sympathy with the rebels have been burned to the ground, while those who escaped were shot down. These are the sober facts, documented by the presence of thousands of refugees in Ethiopia, Uganda and the Congo.

"The real accusation against the missionaries is that they have been silent too long in the face of these atrocities ... Missionaries have long counseled the Sudanese to be patient and non-violent. When all is said, the Sudan is under no obligation to explain to the world why it has expelled 300 missionaries. Its real obligation is to show why it has driven out thousands of its own people."

Unable to make clear plans for the future, with no visa for work in Ethiopia forthcoming, my parents struggled to sort through seventeen years of accumulated goods and personal relationships, knowing that there would probably be no return for them to this place that had become home. Temporarily, they decided to come to Schutz and wait for further developments there.

In actual fact, twenty-seven years after they were forced to leave the Sudan, Dad was able to obtain a visa for a short visit to Khartoum. The country was still being torn apart by civil war, and many southerners had fled the fighting and famine, coming north, only to be trapped in squalid, sprawling refugee camps in the northern desert. Dad was appalled by the dirt and degradation that the people were forced to live in, and knew that the situation in the South must be even worse. But out of that place of poverty and hopelessness, old Shilluk friends came to greet him. He was still to them the Oshoda they had known. Together they shared news from the south, read from the Shilluk New Testament, which had indeed finally been published. They sang hymns from the new Shilluk hymnal, which was now full of truly Shilluk music, rather than Americanized hymns in attempted translation, and expressed the struggle of the people to trust in God in spite of oppression, captivity, homelessness and despair. Then, with great respect, they thanked Dad for the gift of the gospel in their own language, and listened as he refused a translator, and pulled from his memory rusty Shilluk words to preach just as he had done so long ago in Dolieb Hill.

But in 1963, the grief of leaving friends and work unfinished was fresh and the future unknown. So, taking a leap of faith, they left the Sudan and headed for Alexandria.

When they arrived at Schutz, the Schutzites immediately adopted them as "Uncle Bill and Aunt Martha." Mom began to help out with nursing duties, and Dad took on the Boy Scouts, and taught math in the grade school. Morn's letters to Grandma during that time are full of the uncertainty that the future held, and the feeling of being in limbo with things to do on the surface, but nothing to address the underlying anxiety. She does share also her joy in being with her family, though in a unique position where she couldn't establish a real family life. One letter reports that she made 190 filled cookies for the grade school kids. Her grandchildren today can vouch for the value of that gift, as these cookies are now an Adair Thanksgiving tradition.

By the end of the school year the visitor's visa for Egypt had expired and Ethiopia had not opened its arms. Schutz had asked Mom and Dad to stay on as house parents, an offer they were considering with some trepidation. In order to renew their Egyptian visa or apply for a work permit, they had to leave the country and request re-entry, so that summer we took a family vacation to Cyprus.

Chapter Twenty: Hamam

There were both advantages and disadvantages to having my parents at Schutz, but there is certainly nothing better than having your mother there when you are sick. In my sophomore year, just after Mom and Dad arrived at Schutz, I woke up in the middle of the night, heaving my guts up. For the next two days I lay on a cot in my parents' apartment, unable to move without setting off another bout of vomiting, and terrified that I had something deadly. Perhaps it was the dreaded Bilharzia, the scourge of Egypt. Snails that inhabited the nasty water of the canals that ran through the city carried this deadly disease. The sewers were also infected. These same sewers regularly overflowed into the streets of Rue Schutz, so that on trips to the little candy store just outside the Schutz compound, we often had to wade through thick, odorous muck.

I had no idea what the symptoms of Bilharzia were, but I was beginning to think that I surely had it, or something equally serious. When the school doctor, Dr. Aisha, came to examine me, I knew I was truly ill. Then, Mom began to pack, and said that I was going to the mission hospital in Tanta! The train would be too much of an ordeal, she said. We were going by taxi. I was, by that time, too sick and frightened to care how we got there.

I had been to Tanta before, when Miriam was born, and had visited there at the home of the Jamisons, my friend Sandy's family, when she and I had been sent there to have EKG tests done to check on heart murmurs. I remembered touring the hospital after the tests were done, but I had never been admitted to that, or any other, hospital. Fortunately, Mom knew the ropes, and enough Arabic to cope with the Egyptian staff, who did not speak English.

Dr. Jamison came to the room as soon as we started to get settled, having been alerted by a phone call from Schutz. As they drew blood from one arm and hooked up an IV to another, I thoroughly embarrassed myself with continual retching, sending nurses scrambling to get out of the way and find a basin for me.

"Dr. Aisha was right," I heard Dr. Jamison say. "She has a bad case of hepatitis. She is really dehydrated, and will need complete bed rest for a while. You should probably stay with here for a week or so until she stabilizes a little. And don't let her out of bed!"

Mom explained to me a little about hepatitis, which at least was less serious than balharzia, so I was feeling somewhat relieved until she asked if I would like to see how I looked. The yellow eyed, sallow skinned image the mirror showed was less than reassuring. Several days later, I came down with German measles, and added a bright pink rash to the picture! Thank God no one at Schutz could see me then!

After about a week, I had gained a little strength and my appetite began to improve, so Mom felt that she should return to Schutz to pick up my homework. Those first few days I missed her sorely. I was still not supposed to get out of bed, but now I had to rely on the young Egyptian nurses' aides to get what I needed, including the bedpan. The trouble was, no one had told me what the Arabic word for bedpan was. I finally decided that the word for bathroom, hamam, was the best I could do, and with great trepidation, I hit the call buzzer.

When the aide arrived, I timidly stammered, "Hamam, men fudlick (please)," and waited to see if I had been understood. She smiled, and glanced, questioning, at the ceiling. I tried again, "Hamam?" Again she glanced up, raising her brows as if to say, "What do you need that for?" In desperation I repeated it louder, and started to get out of bed and walk to the bathroom. This brought her immediately to my side saying, "Laa, laa laa," (no, no, no)." Smothering giggles, she finally divined my meaning and brought me the bedpan. O blessed relief!

When Dr. Jamison came, I asked him what the word for bed pan was, and told him that I had tried the word for bathroom, and the nurses' aide had left the room in a fit of giggles.

"What word did you use?" he asked. I repeated it, "Hamam."

"Oh," he said, trying not to laugh himself. "It's hamam."

"That's what I said." I told him.

"Well, it's very close," he soothed, but your intonation is wrong. You need to drop the tone at the end instead of raising it. The way you said it, it means pigeon!" No wonder the poor girl kept looking at the ceiling.

After about four weeks in Tanta hospital, Dr. Jamison finally agreed to send me back to school, but I would have to stay on bed rest. I had come to rather enjoy my stay. Every weekend Mom arrived with piles of homework for the week ahead, letters and even pictures from friends and classmates, and very special notes from Dave. I still remember the thrill of opening each one, as well as the agony of what to say in response. The difficulty I always had with talking to boys was neatly circumvented by the written word, so I was anxious to return to Schutz and yet afraid that my newfound ability to communicate with the opposite sex would desert me.

I had managed to keep up with all of my classes except geometry, so under the guise of geometry tutor, Dave visited me daily in the sickroom. Once the math session was over, my room became the headquarters for all who wanted in on a card game. What fun it was to be the center of attention, surrounded nightly by friends of both sexes. Mrs. Bob, the chaplains' wife was truly offended by the fact that males were not only in my bedroom, but sitting all over the bed! I'm sure that I have Mom to thank for allowing the nightly games to continue. That was the last year that Dave was at Schutz, so our precourtship was short lived, but nonetheless sweet. I think I even passed geometry!

Chapter Twenty-One: The Sea

What a marvelous lover of nature my Grandmother Hamilton was! When we returned to the States for good, and she came to live with us, she created her own little world in her bedroom, filling it with all the things she loved most. All across one of the walls surged wave after wave of a blue green sea, crashing in frothy white against gray rocks, spray flung toward the sky and white caps gathering power in the background. I was drawn to that picture, for I had often seen just such a sea in Alexandria.

The Corniche in Alexandria follows the coastline of the Mediterranean Sea for several miles, and marks the joining of the city's edge with the beaches. In places the sand comes almost to the sidewalk, in others there is a short brick wall. Mostly, the beach is easily accessible, though there are rocky sections, which are not so inviting.

After church on Sundays, Schutzites could be seen all along the Corniche, strolling along nonchalantly as couples, publicly acknowledging their attraction, or strung out in happy groups of laughing children. I relished that walk alongside the sea, delighting in the chance to share her many moods.

Sometimes all was serene, the placid water a brilliant sheet of aquamarine, reflecting back the white-hot sunlight and dazzling the eyes. Sometimes gently rounded waves swelled and lifted up crests of white froth, which slipped up on the sand and then withdrew, gently stroking the beach. And there were frenzied days when the wind that grabbed my hair and lifted my skirt, whipped the water into huge breakers that rose menacingly and smashed onto the rocks, sending spray out over the wall and drenching the Corniche from one end to the other.

To watch these changing moods from the safety of the sidewalk was to vicariously experience both the violence and the serenity. To actually swim was to experience an entirely different aspect of the sea. Our first years at Schutz, we were home in the Sudan during the summer months, when swimming in the Mediterranean was safe, but after Mom and Dad were expelled, and came to Schutz, Dad took us regularly to the swimming beaches, along with anyone else who was summering at Schutz.

Although not a powerful swimmer, I had absolute confidence in Dad's ability to rescue me if necessary, and did not hesitate to struggle out some distance from the shore, to explore the reefs. One day, having reached that goal, I clung, breathing heavily, to the reefs, trying not to show too obviously how exhausted the trip had made me. Tim was there ahead of me, perched on the reef with snorkel and fins, and jabbering about how wonderful the underwater landscape was. I was intrigued, though scared. He, however, was determined that I should take a turn, and knowing me well, began to challenge me with comments like: "Well, if you're too scared, then never mind!" He knew me well, still does in fact, and convinced our kids to use the same technique not long ago in Minnesota, to get me into the freezing lake.

Determined to prove to him that I could do it, scared or not, I pulled myself up onto the reef and sat down to work the flippers onto my feet. That part was easy, but the mask gave me a claustrophobic moment or two before I learned not try to breathe through my nose! Finally ready, I took the leap, and immediately found it had been worth the effort. Right under the surface the appeared a sort of underwater jungle, full of life, color and movement. I was mesmerized! It was, however, hard work to swim and remember to breathe properly, and I soon returned to my seat on the reef, and peeled of my equipment so that someone else could explore.

Suddenly, I felt a sharp pain in my right buttock! Thinking I was sitting on a pointed rock, I slid back into the water and headed back to the beach. Halfway there, I began to huff and puff, and then to really struggle for enough breath to reach the shore. Rising panic lent me strength! I ploughed through the water, moving faster than I ever thought was possible. As I stumbled onto the beach, the world was whirling about me, and I could hear myself screaming, "Dad! Dad! I can't breathe!"

The next thing I knew, I was laying on the sand, Dad kneeling beside me yelling, "Yes you can! Breathe! Breathe!" I felt as if a gargantuan wave had slammed me down into the beach, leaving me gasping for air, confused and terrified! Was I dying? I grabbed for Dad, trying to scream, hearing nothing but the blood pounding in my ears, and Dad muttering, "Breathe! Breathe!" I couldn't do it, and then suddenly I could! I felt my flattened lungs inflate, and burst into tears, sobbing with each marvelous inhalation, "I couldn't breathe! I couldn't breathe!"

Dad lifted me up, supporting me as we labored over to the car. Subdued, and still a little frightened, the other kids gathered their towels and followed, whispering to each other, "What happened? Is she okay?"

Staggering up to the car, I tried to slide into the seat, and realized that the right half of my butt felt like it was on fire! Then I remembered the pain I had felt out on the reef. "Something bit me on the seat," I said. Out there on the reef, something stung me!"

"Good grief!" Dad said. "You must have sat on one of those poisonous sea urchins!" This brought titters from my siblings, on who I turned angrily. "It's not funny!" I spat. "It's not a joke not being able to breathe! I thought I was going to die!" We rode back to Schutz in sobered silence. When we got there, Mom operated on my now-swollen behind, and removed the stinger, which had indeed shot me with poison.

For several days I could not sit, or lie down comfortably. As I carried a foam doughnut around with me, so that I could tuck my injured buttock into the doughnut hole, avoiding painful contact with the chair, I began to enjoy all the attention, and to laugh rather weakly at the inevitable jokes and snickers, but I could not forget, and have not still forgotten, the overwhelming terror of fighting so desperately to draw a single breath!

There were many uneventful swims, though to some extent the feel of sun and sand and seaweed was an event in itself. Sometimes, we rented small raft-like boards, which I hesitate to characterize as surfboards, because they were so primitive and clumsy. Most of the time, they did at least float, so that we could paddle out beyond the breakers, and dive into the deep deep waters of the sea. Nothing I have experienced since that time has ever equaled the exhilaration of balancing on that tiny raft and looking out over the spacious expanse of clear blue water. Then, breathing deeply, and diving head first, slicing through the blueness, deep into the chilly depths, then up, up, up, lungs burning, till I burst through the surface, sucking in the clean, warm air, and dashing salty water from my eyes and mouth.

There were often Egyptian lifeguards on the beach, as well as sellers of sesame candy and toffee apples, strolling up and down, calling loud attention to the trays of goodies they balanced on their heads. There was an established system of different colored flags to indicate how safe each beach was for swimming that day. When the waves were rough, or the undertow strong, a black flag flew, and no swimming was allowed. Red meant that you could swim, but at your own risk, and no flag indicated perfect conditions, and a lifeguard on duty. Sometimes when we arrived, ready to swim, and the flag was red, we went on in, since Dad was trained in water safety and rescue technique, and the bigger waves provided an opportunity to body surf.

One rather windy morning, when a red flag flew, Bob, a friend and classmate, and I, had rented a raft, and were battling our way out to sea, trying to get beyond the rough and tumble breakers. We topped one wave, felt a brief moment of triumph, and were body-slammed by the next one, which ripped our raft out from under us!

"Get the raft! Get the raft!" Bob yelled, straining to keep his head above water as the next wave crested behind him. I struck out toward it, reached out, and then struggled to keep a grasp on the slick surface. Just as I pulled myself up on the side, a wave crashed over me again, knocking me silly. Then Bob was there, but even with the two of us, we couldn't get back on and stay there.

Suddenly, above the crash of breakers, we heard frenzied screams, and craned our necks to see a young Egyptian man flailing around and screeching his head off. "He's just faking," said Bob cynically. "If we go over there he'll try to take our raft!" It was certainly no secret that if you allowed yourself to get separated from your raft, someone else would claim it, and it would be "finders keepers."

I glanced doubtfully at Bob, and then back at the young man, who continued to give a very convincing impression of drowning. Dithering in indecision, I weathered the next wave, and emerged from the assault to see Dad barreling past me, swimming faster than I had ever seen him go before! He grabbed the man by the armpits, and was about to demonstrate his Boy Scout lifesaving technique, when he realized that they were directly over a reef, and all the petrified man had to do was stop struggling and put his feet down! Between the rolling of each breaking wave, he could easily have pushed up from the bottom.

Minutes after this revelation, the lifeguard arrived at their side, and together he and Dad dragged the poor man to the beach, where all the sunbathers and the sellers were on their feet, cheering the dramatic rescue!

Knowing the sea first hand, standing in awe under the spray as tons of water crashed against the rocks, floating lazily on a placid surface, or diving deep into the briny depths, such knowledge is a gift of sparkling memory, that touches something spiritual and pure in me, filling me with profound, though enigmatic wonder. Perhaps that is what drew my grandmother to its likeness, surging across the wall of her little room in the middle of land-bound Kansas?

Chapter Twenty-Two: By Deck

At the end of my sophomore year at Schutz the school board asked Mom and Dad to stay on at Schutz as houseparents. How they agonized over the decision. Ethiopia still had not opened its arms to them and they didn't want to return to the States if there was still some way for Dad to complete his translation work. But houseparents? It seemed like more of a responsibility than they thought they were capable of assuming. On the other hand, they could be at Schutz with us, and I only had two years before graduation. Maybe in that time a way would become clear. Finally, they did accept, and prayed that Dad's coworker, Ezekiel, would be able to come to Egypt periodically to work with him. Their temporary Egyptian visa had, meanwhile, expired, so in order to renew it they had to leave the country and apply for reentry, with a work permit for employment at Schutz. That was the summer we took a family vacation to Cyprus.

We began the trip, as we began all out of country expeditions, by sitting in customs, this time at the dock in Alexandria. I looked with some apprehension at the SS Massalia, squatting on the water like some pregnant walrus sunning on a rock. It's squalid, rusted body seemed light years removed from the sleek luxury liners I remembered sailing on in the years before jet travel became affordable. Crossing the ocean in the majestic Queen Mary had, of course, been the epitome of luxury, even in tourist class. But even the more humble vessel, the Independence, upon which I had celebrated my eleventh birthday as we steamed toward New York, seemed distinctly unrelated to this scraggly looking hulk, though generically, both were ships.

Despite the unreassuring appearance of the Massalia, we were all in a state of high anticipation as we stood by the dock, for this trip from Alexandria to Limassol, Cyprus was going to be by deck! As we sat on our hand baggage, wilting in the heat, impatient for Dad to convince the customs officials that he was truly not going to smuggle anything out of Egypt, we watched the available deck space up on the ship dwindle. People were stumbling up the gangplank in droves, dragging and/or shoving humongous loads of variously packaged bundles. Baskets of food, rolls of bedding, clanking collections of cooking utensils, and here and there a live chicken or even a goat. All over the deck, small groups of people squatted, surrounded by jumbles of household goods, among which young children ran wild. Charcoal braziers began to appear, and women bent to the business of making morning tea.

Adding to the sounds of all this burgeoning domesticity was the screaming, cursing chaos of the workers loading the hold. Supervisors ran helter-skelter over the deck, shaking their fists at the crane operators, whose overloaded nets of cargo swung crazily over the heads of all, making people duck with curses and prophecies of dire results every time the creaking machines labored to lift another load.

By the time Dad had completed his negotiations, which had been complicated by his refusal to pay a bribe, and we were allowed on board, the only space not already claimed by squatter's rights was on top of the hold, which was just being closed, the loading completed. We hauled our sleeping bags and other paraphernalia onto the hold doors, and arranged a boundary to the territory we had established. Appointing Mom as guard, we then ran to the prow of the ship to watch as the Massalia was slowly tugged out into the open Mediterranean Sea.

Back at the hold, Mom was beginning to have belated second thoughts about deck travel. Hemmed in on all sides by curious Arabs, she understood enough Arabic to know that everyone was discussing what on earth an American family (who by their standards was more than wealthy) was doing traveling by deck. (She could have told them this was one of her making-memories trips.) She was also nursing a headache, so she tried to ignore everything, and stretched out on a sleeping bag, attempting to relax, an obviously futile enterprise, considering the circumstances.

Restlessly, Mom tried to find a comfortable position, pummeling her pillow into shape, and trying to pretend that her hip was not grinding into the hard wooden planks. Finally, totally dispirited, she turned onto her back, and from the corner of her eye saw a young man who had laid out his bedroll nearby, reach out and gather up some of our pillows with which we had marked our perimeter. Her notorious temper flared. Infuriated, she waited until he began to nestle into a comfortable nest and WHAP! She pulled the pillows out from under his head, watching with great satisfaction as it landed with a thump against the wooden deck!

The Middle Eastern sense of drama was definitely satisfied as the onlookers took sides, engaging if furious arguments, in several languages, as to who was right and who was wronged. Mom, now totally embarrassed, sat sheepishly quiet in the eye of the storm.

When the babble finally began to subside, it was lunchtime. A breeze was starting to roughen the seas, making the tubby Massalia bob about like an apple in a tub at Halloween. We had planned to eat with the crew, but Dad was the only one with any appetite. The rest of us were hovering by the railing, fighting off nausea, closing our eyes to shut out the dipping of the horizon, and praying that the fresh sea air would restore equilibrium.

The sight of hordes of seasick peasants, crouched up and down the railing, bare feet wading in rivulets of each other's vomit, was enough to make even the strongest stomach lurch! We passed a very restless night. By morning, the sea was calm, and the Massalia chugged along, leaving a gorgeous white wake on the glassy surface.

Gwen and I went in search of a restroom. After several wrong turns, we located it by the stench that oozed from the door out into the hallway. Gingerly, we opened it. There were the stalls, but between them and us, the floor was covered with an inch of water, upon which globs of vomit and other unrecognizable tidbits floated. Speechless, we stared at the mess. "I have to go really bad!" Gwen stammered.

"Me too!" I muttered, afraid to open my mouth lest I add to the globs glistening at my feet. "Hold your breath and run for it," I gasped, and we dashed on tiptoe through the muck.

As we left the stalls, we came face to face with a portly Arab man, ankle deep in slimy goo, blithely shaving in front of the mirror. We both let out a shriek, turned beet red, and stumbled for the door, while he stood there grinning, and bellowing "Malish! Malish!" (the standard Arab response to any difficult or embarrassing situation, "Never mind!").

Back on deck, Gwen and I stammered out our story. Apparently we had not entered the men's room by mistake. Deck travelers were assigned only one bathroom, shared by all. At that point I would have traded this memory-making experience for a nice sedate trip in a cabin. It was with some relief that, several hours later, I sighted the island of Cyprus.

Chapter Twenty-Three: Cyprus

The dock in the port city of Limassol, Cyprus, did not appear much different from the one in Alexandria. There were the same salty sea-weed smells, the same debilitating heat, chaotic crowds of people from all over the Middle East, deeply involved in intense conversations and arguments that erupted in fistfights, and the same endless waiting in the middle of it all for Dad to deal with the customs officials. "What's so great about a vacation in Cyprus?" I thought in disappointment.

Once we were finally allowed to proceed beyond the dock, and had loaded all of our stuff into two taxis, heading for the town of Troodos, which the camp we were to stay at was located near, things became much more interesting. Troodos was up in the mountains, and apparently the only way to get there was over a poorly paved road, that didn't seem wide enough for even one vehicle. Heaven forbid we should meet one coming the opposite way! None of this seemed to affect the speed with which the taxi drivers negotiated one hairpin turn after another. On the left of us was solid rock mountainside, on the right, an open chasm that grew deeper and deeper as we continued to climb. Afraid to look to either side, with no reassurance offered by looking ahead at what was to come, I finally buried my head in my arms, closed my eyes, and prayed for a miracle. "Dear God, HELP!"

An hour and a half later, I felt the pace begin to slow and looked up. We had entered an incredible pine forest unlike anything I had ever seen. It was almost worth the preceding terror. The pungent pine scent prickled my nose as I breathed in the crisp, cool mountain air, which seemed to carry with it a sense of quiet serenity that both soothed and exhilarated me. We turned off the pavement and followed a rocky road up to the camp. Suddenly shrouded in the cool shady greenness of the forest, I felt as if some magic time warp had transported me to another world and time.

There was a large guesthouse, in which a family that we knew slightly was staying, and some distance from that two huge tents were set up among the trees. These were our accommodations for the next six weeks, and never having been camping before, we thought they were marvelous!

Although this was a deluxe camping set up, there was still plenty of work to haul water for cooking, etc. But there was also plenty of time for fun. We were surrounded by opportunities for hiking and exploring through the forest, and up the road a mile or so in the little town of Troodos.

Exulting in the freedom to roam around on our own, Tim and I often took off together on mini-expeditions. One day, we discovered a large area of the mountainside that had apparently been burned. The blackened treeless ground was loose and stony. In some places, small avalanches of dirt and rocks had left long scrapes down the mountainside that looked like scars not yet totally healed.

Intrigued, we left the road to clamber over the area, slipping and sliding as we struggled to the top of a rise and stopped to look around. In a pile of trash several feet below us, I saw a couple of cardboard boxes. "Hey Tim, let's use those boxes for sleds!" I said. "This stuff is so loose, I bet we could slide all the way to the bottom!"

"Wow! I bet we could!" he agreed, and began to scramble down to where they were. "This is great! We can open these up, sit on them, and shove off!"

It took a little while to suit action to words, but oh what a ride we had! It was both steeper and looser than we had anticipated! Faster, faster, and faster we went, almost catching air as we whizzed over bumps and branches that were in our path. Screeching with glee, and not a little fear, I hit a rock, turned sideways, struggled to right myself and then, "Yeaow!!" My cardboard slid out from under me and came to a stop, while I continued to hurtle down the mountainside, literally hanging in there by the seat of my pants! By the time I got myself stopped, I had left a large portion of my pants and underpants, not to mention several layers of skin, behind me.

Tim, his cardboard still intact, was gleefully sliding down after me, oblivious to my predicament. "Whew! This is great!" he said, digging his feet into the dirt and coming to a perfect stop. "Let's do it again!"

Wordlessly, I turned to show him my injured backside. "How am I going to get home?" I wailed. "I can't walk down the road with a big hole in my pants!"

"Whoa! You're bleeding too you know," he said.

I turned in circles like a dog chasing its tail, trying to inspect the damage, and struggled against tears as I envisioned myself with my backside exposed to the world, walking along the road. What if a jeep load of soldiers from the RAF station in Troodos should come up behind us!? Seeing that I was both embarrassed and hurting, Tim soberly offered to walk right behind me, but the closer we came to road the more upset I became. Then I hit upon a partial solution. "Wait here," I said, and went behind some bushes, where I took my pants off and turned my underwear around, so that at least no skin was showing through the ruined seat. Even so, when we reached the road, I kept one eye on Tim to be sure he was covering my backside. It was still a long and uncomfortable walk home.

On other, less eventful jaunts, we explored the area as a family, renting a car, taking a picnic, and making a day of it. On one particularly gorgeous day, we stopped by a small lake. We had come prepared to swim, having heard that there were places allowing this, and decided it would be great fun to just jump in and swim to the other side, while Mom drove the car around. Dad was game, so we rushed ahead and plunged right in! Never before or since, have I experienced such bone chilling cold. I thought my heart and lungs had been flash frozen! We had not realized what altitude does to still deep water!

We also found out that summer that a thunderstorm in the mountains was very different from one on the savannah or by the ocean. You couldn't watch them coming as you could when you could see to the horizon. And they seemed to come so suddenly and with such ferocity, the thunder and lightning somehow amplified by the forest. During one such storm, a lightning bolt struck a tree just outside our tent, with a blazing ball of fire that split the tree halfway down the trunk, and a clap of thunder that left our ears ringing for hours afterward!

It was a very special time for me that summer in Cyprus, tucked away in the forest with my family. The concern about the coming junior year, with the accompanying knowledge that my career as a Schutzite could not go on forever, still lay like a slumbering dragon just below the surface of my mind. But it was a quiescent threat, overlaid with experiences of the immediate presence of nature's beauty, and the great gift of family togetherness, which was heightened by a previous knowledge of what it meant to be apart.

Chapter Twenty-Four: Celebration!

The most wonderful things about celebrations at our house was the excitement of having company! How we loved it when other mission families came to see us! When we got to be the hosts of a gathering, it was an extra special time because usually, gatherings were held in Malakal, where three families were stationed, and we would travel there by boat, or by truck, depending on whether it was rainy season, and we were "mudded in" or not.

The clay soil made it impossible to travel by truck for months at a time. I can remember several times when Dad thought things were dry enough, and ended up on his back under the truck for up to four hours, trying to pry the wheels loose from the foot deep, grainy glue, and ending up so covered with the stuff that the driver's seat soon looked almost as bad as the outside of the truck did.

For hours before the ETA (estimated time of arrival) we would be standing out on the verandah, hoping to be the first to hear the whine of the Evinrude engine. Then the race was on to be first at the banks of the Sobat, screaming out a happy welcome.

Since my birthday was in the summer, I *always* got to celebrate at home, even after I started going to Schutz. I was the only one for whom this was true, and it was a position I cherished.

Gift giving did not get much emphasis at our celebrations because there was really no place to shop for anything special, so food and friends were the important things. The menu I remember having most often was juicy thick hamburgers on homemade buns. Then Mom would pull out all the stops, make homemade potato chips and freeze ice in every available container in the tiny little freezer of the kerosene powered fridge so that Dad could power up the old hand cranked ice cream freezer. Ah … Ambrosia!

It was never assumed that there would be birthday cake, since this depended on whether or not we had been able to get fresh eggs recently. Added to the limited availability was the more than likely chance that not all of the eggs we were able to purchase would actually be good. We tested each one in a pan of water, looking for the floaters, which would definitely be rotten.

Before long, however, the word got out that if you boiled the eggs before you took them to Dandwong, they would sink to the bottom, and pass the test, even if they were rotten. One year, when no one showed up with eggs for sale, Mom created an eggless chocolate pie, which is certainly a birthday treat I will never forget. Even then, I appreciated the feeling of being special enough for Mom to find a way to have celebratory food.

Some summers, we were traveling from Sudan to the States in July, and then we would celebrate in transit. I'll never forget the birthday bash aboard the ocean liner, the Independence. The whole dining room participated in cheering and singing Happy Birthday, as I blew out the candles on a marvelous chocolate on chocolate cake!

Often, a party at our house would include a presentation of the latest song that Dad had modified, or skit that Mom had found for us to perform. Then, the adults would play Rook. (No games with a regular deck please, since they were used for gambling.) What a comforting vision it is: those beloved adults gathered with laughter around the card table, in the lovely yellow light of the primus lamp. Around the edge of the group, we kids would hover, enjoying the feeling of extended family as we tried to learn the rudiments of the game. What a coming of age it was when we were considered old enough to actually play!

At Christmas, there was usually just our family, so it was not as exciting as other celebrations. I remember decorating a thorn tree, and having special Church services. I don't think Dad dressed like Santa, though apparently my grandfather did when they were at Nasir, and scared the houseboys half to death! Once we began attending Schutz, we didn't get to come home for Christmas, so it definitely lost its luster. The first time Ed and I had to stay with a mission family at the girl's School in Cairo it was horrible! They did the best they could, and I do remember hearing the *Messiah* for the first time, but we were so homesick that we could barely mope through the day, trying mightily to be grateful and hating every minute.

The year of the evacuation, we were home for Christmas, and our friends from Schutz who Mom was schooling with us were there too; a perfect set up. We performed the age-old nativity story, sang all the glorious Christmas songs and of course, watched the Rook game.

After Mom and Dad came up to Schutz, my summer birthday celebrations took on new life. One year, we gathered all the Schutzites who were summering at Sidi Bishr, and took a picnic to the beach at Agamy. We swam, had sack races and games on the beach, and ate the tastiest rotisserie chicken I have ever had! Mom picked it up at a restaurant in Alex and I have tried and tried to reproduce the flavor, with no success. Perhaps it is like so many memories. They become better with each telling, and can never be accurately reproduced again.

I know that it was my mother who made sure that so many of our experiences would be things we would remember. She worked hard at creating memorable events for us, and all of us are so very very grateful to her for the magical feelings which that gift still brings to us. I am amazed how powerful many of those feelings and images still are, so that even though I can never truly go back in time and be home in Africa, in my mind I can summon up those individual moments and savor them for the rest of my life.

Chapter Twenty-Five: The Nile Hilton

"Room service? What is room service?" I said to Sandy. She shook her head, obviously as mystified as I was. We turned to Miss Bode, who smiled at our ignorance. "It's like breakfast in bed," she said. You call down to the hotel kitchen and order whatever you want, and the waiter brings it right up to your room! "Wow!" Neither of us had ever stayed in a place posh enough to offer room service!

We were sitting on the balcony of a room at the Nile Hilton, still in our nightgowns, looking out over the Nile River as it flowed through Cairo, with its busy traffic of small sailboats and larger, houseboat-like feluccas, wondering how we got to be the lucky ones. We were both seniors that year, and each, in our own way, having a difficult time. Miss Bode was teaching the advanced English class we were taking, and though she worked us hard, making us struggle and "think, think, think." she also cared about how we were doing outside class. When she offered to take us to Cairo for the weekend, we were thrilled!

The Nile Hilton was the classiest place either of us had ever stayed in. The Hilton chain of hotels was fairly new at the time, and was to us luxurious beyond belief. The limited budget of a missionary family did not stretch to include stays in 4 star hotels!

That evening, as we walked into the dining room, we were overwhelmed at the brocaded glory of the drapes and carpet, and the elegantly appointed tables. Everywhere we looked, sufrages in brilliantly while galabias , red velvet tarbooshes and cummerbunds were waiting to provide for every comfort. The natural hospitality of the Egyptian people was on display as they attended to the guests.

Within seconds of entering the room, we had our own retinue of waiters pulling out our chairs, filling our glasses, spreading snowy napkins on our laps, and bowing as they offered menus and asked in heavily accented English what we would like. In equally awkward Arabic, Sandy and I thanked them, "Shookran, shookran," and then looked to Miss Bode, who was fluent in the language.

There was, fortunately, a menu in English. Shish kabobs, kufta, rice pilaf, and aash baladi with tahini sauce were just the beginning. They also offered "American" gamoosa burgers and an Egyptain facsimile of french fries, but we were partial to Egyptian specialties, and after some agonizing, we made our choices. Unused to such exalted surroundings, we were very much on our best behavior, trying to seem adult, rather than the overawed teenagers we knew ourselves to be.

As I minded my manners, eating slowly and trying not to stare at the other guests, I felt something nudge my foot under the table. Embarrassed at bumping Sandy, or worse, Miss Bode, I tucked my feet under my chair, and focused on my food. Bump! There it was again! Somewhat flummoxed, I tried to decide what to do with my feet, and then started in surprise as a huge cat stalked out from under my chair, and haughtily looked around as if it were the proprietor of the place, and wondered what on earth we were doing there. It turned, looked up, and suddenly leaped onto the table in front of me, causing me to stifle a shriek of protest, and back my chair away. Immune to the furor I was creating, it paraded daintily around the table, while we gaped in horror, hoping it would not start eating from our plates!

By this time, the entire dining room was watching, goggle-eyed, and a phalanx of waiters bore down on us, flapping napkins and yelling, "Imshee! Imshee me henna!" The cat fluffed up to twice its size, hissed, yowled like a banshee, and streaked from the table to the floor, leaving havoc in its wake as people scattered. It made a grab for the drapes, fell, and finally found the door, narrowly missing a line of sufragees bearing fully laden trays.

"Malish. Malish." The waiters tried to sooth everyone with the old Egyptian panacea, "Never mind, never mind." "Please return to your dinner." We, however, seeing cat hair from one end of the table to the other, decided we had best retire before hilarity got the better of us, and stumbled, giggling, to the door, leaving Miss Bode to deal with the apologetic staff.

Chapter Twenty-Six: Graduation

My last years at Schutz were difficult in many ways, partly because I began to realize that Schutz, as I knew it, was changing, and because everything I did was tarnished by my growing uncertainty about what leaving Schutz would mean. Schutz had been my life for years; all I wanted, all I needed, all I knew. The great unknown of the future loomed, and it terrified me! In 1999, as many Schutzites gathered in Pennsylvania to celebrate the 75th anniversary of the school, many of us struggled to put into words what that special Schutz mystique was, which had touched so many of us. Three hundred and fifty people, spanning all ages, gathered for a weekend to share memories and ponder that question. What did it mean then, what does it mean now to have been a Schutzite?

Community was part of what we had. It is an inherently nebulous concept, and yet, when experienced it takes on a sort of miraculous aura, which is very deep and very real. There is a feeling for members of a community of safety and of belonging. At Schutz, away from our own families, this was intense, and something we strongly clung to. Part of the deep and searing pain of leaving Schutz was facing the loss of this community experience, which we had taken for granted, until we realized we could lose it. In addition, during the time I was at Schutz, there was definitely a spirit which was more than just a blending of human consciousness. Many of the staff working there then, including my own parents, considered their positions to be sacred responsibilities, and sought God's presence in their work and in the lives of the children entrusted to them. Although this began to change during my last years, most of the years I spent there were influenced by this approach.

My inability to deal with the emotional pain of leaving Schutz sometimes made me physically ill. I very nearly missed my own graduation ceremony, huddled over the toilet, cold, shivering and nauseous. At the very last minute I sidled into my seat to receive my diploma. Every time I look at pictures of myself at graduation, in my elegant brocade dress which Mom had had specially made, I see a pasty face and scraggly hair, my agony over leaving Schutz captured on film.

The summer after I graduated, we left Schutz and Africa, for good. Dad was going to Kenya to work with the Shilluk pastor, Ezekiel on finishing the translation of the New Testament into Shilluk. The rest of us were headed for the States. We sailed to Beirut, and stayed there overnight before separating. I don't remember my mother crying when we left Alexandria, but she was overwhelmed that night in Beirut. She too, was leaving behind lives that we had loved, and I suspect that she was as unsure of the future as I was. Although I do think that she understood the importance of Dad's translation work, and the urgency he felt to complete it so that it could reach the Shilluk people, she was still facing a difficult transition, and she was going to have to do it alone.

Supper was gloomy. What I ordered for my last Middle Eastern meal, I don't remember, but Dad had slimy seaweed and cow slobber (mulakeeya). Memories of that evening are permeated with the overpowering aroma of garlic and the taste of bile in the back of my mouth as I tried not to gag. Perhaps it's symbolic, for certainly, leaving Africa sickened me. Learning to face the unknown without fear takes a willingness to grow which was a long time in coming for me.

Coming to terms with my past has also been a slow journey. My memories have floated like a smoky aura shrouding my whole being all these years. Often I have yearned to snatch them to me, and give them a form much more substantial. Sometimes, I've wished that the fresh breeze of change and growth would blow them clean away, and I could then forget the times I felt so different from American children raised in "normal" families.

It seems right that as I write this, I am vacationing with friends on an island in northern Minnesota, immersed in an ambience much like that I grew up in. For here are Mary and Monte, still to me aunt and uncle, though we share no common bloodline. Mary lived at Dolieb Hill, down the path from us at "The Palms," and it was there that Monte came to court her.

I remember well the romance of their wedding, the bride with garlands of delicately scented orange blossoms in her hair, and the church overflowing with the gathered native community intermingled with mission families for Malakal, Obel, and Dolieb Hill. A dream wedding!

On every side, as I sit out on the porch, I am caressed by reminders, symbols that sharpen the focus on dormant feelings and illuminate experiences that had faded with time. I hear the whine of an outboard motor, and remember standing on the veranda at Dolieb Hill with my nose pressed to the screen, stretching on my tiptoes in anticipation. For that sound was a herald of good times. Either Dad was returning from a trip, or company was arriving!

I light the camp stove, and lift the old black box of an oven onto it. I smile enigmatically, for Debbie and her boys are vociferous in their disbelief that the contraption will work. But I remember. Remember baking my first batch of cookies in an oven that could have been its twin.

I trek up to the outhouse, and sit gingerly over the deep stink hole, remembering the bucket that sat beneath a similar perch at Atar, and how I hurried to get done in case the man whose job it was to empty it should suddenly appear and snatch it through the trap door as I sat there.

I light the lamps, smelling the kerosene, and thinking of the nightly ritual of lamp lighting. I see my family gathered around the little pump organ, the yellow circle of light pushing back the darkness, and enclosing us in warm communion.

It is good to remember, for I have made peace with my heritage now, and can accept the gifts it holds, and take them with me on the continuing journey. Gifts of family unity and extended family circle. Gifts of laughter and courage and deep sorrow. Gifts offered for continued growth. Life-supporting gifts for the Daughter of the Palms.

Sudan Background

Military regimes favoring Islamic-oriented governments have dominated national politics since independence from the UK in 1956. Sudan has been embroiled in a civil war for all but 10 years of this period (1972-82). The wars are rooted in northern economic, political, and social domination of the non-Muslim, non-Arab southern Sudanese. Since 1983, the war and the war-related famine-related effects have led to more than 2 million deaths and over 4 million people displaced. The ruling regime is a mixture of military elite and an Islamist party that came into power in a 1989 coup. Some northern opposition parties have made common cause with the southern rebels and entered the war as a part of an anti-government alliance. Peace talks gained momentum in 2002-03 with the signing of several accords, including a cease-fire agreement. Recently, agreement has been made for a shared gov't between north and south for six years, at which time the south may decide to secede.

Forgotten People: Shilluk Kingdom of Sudan

11/18/2004

The majority of the displaced persons are living out in the cold, hiding in the swampy areas and in nearby forested areas. During the attacks on their villages, food granaries and grass for thatching was (sic) also burnt to the ground.

ACT Appeal, October 15, 2004

Why are the People of the Shilluk Kingdom Forgotten?

The world's attention is currently fixed on the humanitarian crisis in Darfur in western Sudan where over one million people have been internally displaced and have become targets of rape and systematic killings by government-backed militias. The Shilluk live in southern Sudan, which has been relatively peaceful since a cease fire agreement in 2002 between the government and the rebel group, the SPLA. However, during the last year, the Kingdom of Shilluk has become a combat zone among competing groups.

The People and the Land
Sudan is Africa's largest country. Sudan has been plagued with civil war since gaining independence from Great Britain in 1956, particularly from 1963 to 1971 and again from the mid-1980s to the present. The nation is divided by cultural and political differences with a small elite population in the north, predominantly Arab in culture, holding political power over the rest of the country. The longest-running conflict in Africa has been waged between the government in Khartoum and the Sudanese People's Liberation Movement/Army (SPLM/A) from southern Sudan.

Political, religious, and ethnic differences are at the center of the protracted civil war that has displaced approximately 4 million people, mostly southerners. The people of the Shilluk Kingdom are one of many ethnic groups in the south impacted by the conflict.

The Shilluk, or the Chollo as they refer to themselves, are Nilotic people who live near the banks of the White Nile River in the Upper Nile region centered around the city of Malakal. They number about 600,000 and are the third most numerous ethnic group in the south after the Dinka and Nuer. Living near the Nile, the Shilluk rely on agriculture, livestock, and fishing for their livelihood. The majority of the Shilluk are Christians, while a small number continue to practice their indigenous religion. Unlike most other ethnic groups in southern Sudan the Shilluk are ruled by a single political/religious figure, and thus their territory is called a kingdom.

Anatomy of the Crisis
The Kingdom of Shilluk remained mostly on the sidelines during the long civil war between SPLA on one side and the Sudanese National Army and government-backed militia groups on the other. Armed conflict broke out in October 2003 when a political leader and former government loyalist, Lam Akol, rejoined the SPLA after breaking away from the movement a decade ago. Fearing that Akol's departure signaled a loss of key strategic areas in the Shilluk Kingdom, the Sudanese government and the militia attacked the SPLA

and loyalists to Akol who were attempting to secure areas previously under his control.

The attacks intensified in 2004 when government supported militias began attacking villages along the White Nile. Between 50,000 and 120,000 people are estimated to have been displaced in the Kingdom, of whom 26,000 have taken refuge in the city of Malakal. Recent information is that the Government is strengthening its garrisons in and near Shilluk and bringing in and arming additional militias. Some observers speculate that this could be the prelude to a dry-season offensive by the government.

Humanitarian Conditions and the International Response

Today, Malakal, the largest city of the Shilluk Kingdom, is overcrowded with internally displaced people and the countryside is dotted with burned homes and villages. As a consequence of the attacks, Shilluk, which is normally self-sufficient in food, is facing serious food shortages.

The UN is only present in Melakal and the World Food Programme (WFP) has been only able to deliver food sporadically due to insecure conditions. The planting season for crops was disrupted by the violence, thus necessitating increased food aid in the future. Shelter materials, medicines, mosquito nets and other non-food items are in short supply. In most of southern Sudan, two years of relative peace have permitted people to begin to rebuild their lives and livelihoods, but in Shilluk conditions have grown worse.

Refugees International Action and Recommendations

Refugees International visited southern Sudan and the Nuba Mountains in October 2004 to assess humanitarian conditions. Although the humanitarian situation in most of Southern Sudan has improved since the 2002 cease fire, it is one of the poorest regions of the world and the people still rely on international aid for survival.

Peace talks between the government of Sudan and the SPLA will soon be reconvened in Nairobi, Kenya and, hopefully, a peace agreement will be reached which will result in a cessation of conflict in Shilluk and other embattled areas. However, it is also possible that the talks will fail and war will be renewed between the north and south of Sudan. As Shilluk is on the border between north and south a renewed conflict could be disastrous for its people.

Refugees International, therefore, recommends that:
- The international community and the United Nations Security Council give their highest priority to fostering a peace agreement between the government of Sudan and the SPLA, including a cessation of hostilities in the Kingdom of Shilluk.
- The U.S. funded Civilian Protection Monitoring Team (CPMT) continue to monitor and report human rights abuses in Shilluk.
- International aid agencies monitor the humanitarian situation in Shilluk closely and increase food and other assistance as needed. As the crop season has been interrupted by conflict, hunger could become worse in Shilluk in the first few months of 2005.

McCall-Pierpaoli Fellow Yodit Fitigu prepared this report, with assistance from Senior Advocate Larry Thompson, who just returned from a mission to southern Sudan.

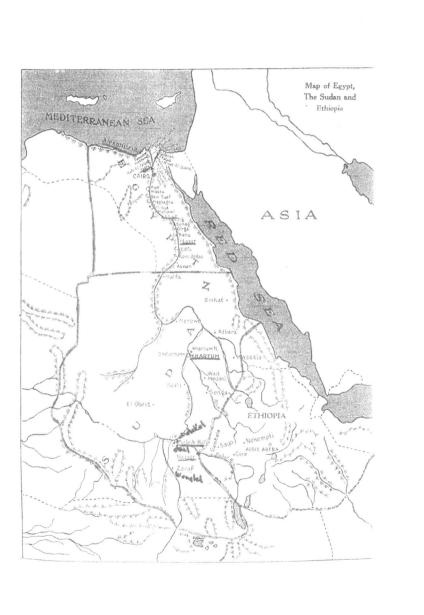

Map of Egypt,
The Sudan and
Ethiopia

MEDITERRANEAN SEA

Alexandria

CAIRO

ASIA

RED SEA

Wasta
Beni Suef
Maghagha
Minya
Mallawi
Suhag
Girga
Kena
Luxor
Edfu
Kom Ombo
Aswan

Halfa

Sinkat

Menowe

Atbara

Khartum N.
Omdurman KHARTUM

Kasala

Wad
Medani

Kosti

Senga

El Obeid

ETHIOPIA

Nekempti

ADDIS ABEBA

Gore

Gambela

Sobat R.

Nasser

Zeraf